P9-DCV-802

Citizenship: A Very Short Introduction

VERY SHORT INTRODUCTIONS are for anyone wanting a stimulating and accessible way into a new subject. They are written by experts, and have been translated into more than 45 different languages.

The series began in 1995, and now covers a wide variety of topics in every discipline. The VSI library now contains over 500 volumes—a Very Short Introduction to everything from Psychology and Philosophy of Science to American History and Relativity—and continues to grow in every subject area.

Titles in the series include the following:

Richard Bellamy

CITIZENSHIP

A Very Short Introduction

OXFORD
UNIVERSITY PRESS

OXFORD
UNIVERSITY PRESS

Great Clarendon Street, Oxford OX2 6DP

Oxford University Press is a department of the University of Oxford.
It furthers the University's objective of excellence in research, scholarship,
and education by publishing worldwide in

Oxford New York

Auckland Cape Town Dar es Salaam Hong Kong Karachi
Kuala Lumpur Madrid Melbourne Mexico City Nairobi
New Delhi Shanghai Taipei Toronto

With offices in

Argentina Austria Brazil Chile Czech Republic France Greece
Guatemala Hungary Italy Japan Poland Portugal Singapore
South Korea Switzerland Thailand Turkey Ukraine Vietnam

Oxford is a registered trade mark of Oxford University Press
in the UK and in certain other countries

Published in the United States
by Oxford University Press Inc., New York

© Richard Bellamy 2008

The moral rights of the author have been asserted
Database right Oxford University Press (maker)

First Published 2008

All rights reserved. No part of this publication may be reproduced,
stored in a retrieval system, or transmitted, in any form or by any means,
without the prior permission in writing of Oxford University Press,
or as expressly permitted by law, or under terms agreed with the appropriate
reprographics rights organization. Enquiries concerning reproduction
outside the scope of the above should be sent to the Rights Department,
Oxford University Press, at the address above

You must not circulate this book in any other binding or cover
and you must impose the same condition on any acquirer

British Library Cataloguing in Publication Data

Data available

Library of Congress Cataloging in Publication Data

Bellamy, Richard (Richard Paul)
Citizenship : a very short introduction / Richard Bellamy.
p. cm.
Includes index.
ISBN 978–0–19–280253–8
1. Citizenship. I. Title.
JF801.B454 2008
323.6–dc22   2008031644

ISBN 978–0–19–280253–8

Impression: 14

Typeset by SPI Publisher Services, Pondicherry, India

Printed and bound by
CPI Group (UK) Ltd, Croydon, CR0 4YY

Contents

Preface

There are many excellent general introductions to citizenship, but to my mind most have a tendency to suffer from one or more of the following three shortcomings. First, they are written either by academics who employ too much jargon to appeal to the general reader, or by non-academics who ignore or are unaware of the latest research on the topic. Second, they focus on the social, moral, or legal aspects of citizenship at the expense of its political dimension. Third, they offer a somewhat linear view of the history of citizenship as a steady progress from ancient Greece to contemporary notions of cosmopolitan citizenship, passing over the many problems in transferring ideas and assumptions that were indeed largely fashioned in the distant past and applying them today. In this book, I have tried to offer something of a corrective to each of these failings. My aims have been, first, to present some of the latest scholarship on citizenship in an accessible way; second, to highlight the irreducibly political nature of citizenship; and third, to explore some of the challenges confronting the very possibility of citizenship today.

I have been greatly helped in this task by the students at Edinburgh, UEA, Reading, Essex, and UCL who have taken the various courses on democracy and citizenship that I have taught over the past 25 years, and the many PhD students whose research on these issues I have supervised. I am also grateful to various friends, family, and colleagues past and present for the numerous discussions about the meaning and nature of citizenship that have shaped the arguments of this book – particularly Malcolm Anderson, Luca Baccelli, Nigel and Steve Bellamy, Pietro Costa, Bernard Crick, Alan Cromartie, Amy and Louise Dominian, John Greenaway, Richard Gunn, Chris Hilson, Barry Holden, the late Martin Hollis, Cécile Laborde, Andrew Mason, Kate Nash, Aletta Norval, Tim O'Hagan, Sarah Playden, Emilio Santoro, Alan Scott, Jo Shaw, Niamh Nic Shuibhne, John Street, Carl Stychin, Jim Tully, Alex Warleigh-Lack, Albert Weale, Andrew Williams, and Danilo Zolo. A special mention is owed to Dario Castiglione, who has not only debated these issues with me during the course of more than a decade's collaboration on diverse research projects dealing with EU citizenship, but also kindly agreed to read and comment on an early draft, saving me from several errors in the process. Last but far from least, I am extremely grateful to the staff at Oxford University Press, particularly James Thompson for hassling me to complete the book, Andrea Keegan – the commissioning editor – for her helpful comments on how I might make it more accessible for a general readership, and Deborah Protheroe for helping me locate the pictures.

List of illustrations

The publisher and the author apologize for any errors or omissions in the above list. If contacted they will be pleased to rectify these at the earliest opportunity.

Chapter 1
What is citizenship, and why does it matter?

Interest in citizenship has never been higher. Politicians of all stripes stress its importance, as do church leaders, captains of industry, and every kind of campaigning group – from those supporting global causes, such as tackling world poverty, to others with a largely local focus, such as combating neighbourhood crime. Governments across the world have promoted the teaching of citizenship in schools and universities, and introduced citizenship tests for immigrants seeking to become naturalized citizens. Types of citizenship proliferate continuously, from dual and transnational citizenship, to corporate citizenship and global citizenship. Whatever the problem – be it the decline in voting, increasing numbers of teenage pregnancies, or climate change – someone has canvassed the revitalization of citizenship as part of the solution.

The sheer variety and range of these different uses of citizenship can be somewhat baffling. Historically, citizenship has been linked to the privileges of membership of a particular kind of political community – one in which those who enjoy a certain status are entitled to participate on an equal basis with their fellow citizens in making the collective decisions that regulate social life. In other words, citizenship has gone hand in hand with political participation in some form of democracy – most especially, the right to vote. The various new forms of citizenship are often put forward as alternatives to this traditional account with its narrow political focus. Yet, though justified in some respects, to expand citizenship too much, so that it comes to encompass people's rights and duties in all their dealings with others, potentially obscures its important and distinctive role as a specific kind of political relationship. Citizenship is different not only to other types of political affiliation, such as subjecthood in monarchies or dictatorships, but also to other kinds of social relationship, such as being a parent, a friend, a partner, a neighbour, a colleague, or a customer.

Over time, the nature of the democratic political community and the qualities needed to be a citizen has changed. The city states of ancient Greece, which first gave rise to the notion of citizenship, were quite different to the ancient Roman republic or the city states of Renaissance Italy, and all differed tremendously from the nation states that emerged in the late 18th and early 19th centuries and that still provide the primary context for citizenship today. In large part, the contemporary concern with citizenship can be seen as reflecting the view that we are currently witnessing a further transformation of political community, and so of citizenship, produced by the twin and related impacts of globalization and multiculturalism. In different ways, these two social processes are testing the capacity of nation states to coordinate and define the collective lives of their citizens, altering the very character of citizenship along the way.

These developments and their consequences for citizenship provide the central theme of this book. The rest of this chapter sets the scene and lays out the book's agenda. I shall start by looking at why citizenship is important and needs to be understood in political terms, then move on to a more precise definition of citizenship, and conclude by noting some of the challenges it faces – both in general, and in the specific circumstances confronting contemporary societies.

Why political citizenship?

Citizenship has traditionally referred to a particular set of political practices involving specific public rights and duties with respect to a given political community. Broadening its meaning to encompass human relations generally detracts from the importance of the distinctively political tasks citizens perform to shape and sustain the collective life of the community. Without doubt, the commonest and most crucial of these tasks is involvement in the democratic process – primarily by voting, but also by speaking out, campaigning in various ways, and standing for office. Whether citizens participate or not, the fact that they can do so colours how they regard their other responsibilities, such as abiding by those democratically passed laws they disagree with, paying taxes, doing military service, and so on. It also provides the most effective mechanism for them to promote their collective interests and encourage their political rulers to pursue the public's good rather than their own.

Democratic citizenship is as rare as it is important. At present, only around 120 of the world's countries, or approximately 64% of the total, are electoral democracies in the meaningful sense of voters having a realistic chance of changing the incumbent government for a set of politicians more to their taste. Indeed, a mere 22 of the world's existing democracies have been continuously democratic in this sense for a period of 50 years or more. And though the number of working democracies has steadily if slowly grown since the Second World War, voter turnout in established democracies has experienced an equally slow but steady decline. For example, turnout in the United States in the period 1945 to 2005 has decreased by 13.8% from the high of 62.8% of eligible voters in 1960 to the low of 49.0% in 1996, and in the UK turnout has gone down by 24.2% from the high of 83.6% in 1950 to the low of 59.4% in 2001. True, as elsewhere, both countries have experienced considerable fluctuations between highs and lows over the past 60 years, depending on how contested or important voters felt the election to be, while in some countries voting levels have remained extremely robust, with Sweden, for example, experiencing a comparatively very modest low of 77.4% in 1958 and a staggering high of 91.8% in 1976. The general downward trend is nevertheless undeniable. Yet, despite citizens expressing increasing dissatisfaction with the democratic arrangements of their countries, they continue to approve of democracy itself. The World Values Survey of 2000–2 found that 89% of respondents in the US regarded democracy as a 'good system of government' and 87% the 'best', while in the UK 87% thought it 'good' and 78% the 'best' (in Sweden it was 97% and 94% respectively). Whatever the perceived or real shortcomings of most democratic systems, therefore, most members of democratic countries seem to accept that democracy matters and that it is the prospect of influencing government policy according to reasonably fair rules and on a more or less equal basis with others that forms the distinguishing mark of the citizen. In those countries where people lack this crucial opportunity, they are at best guests and at worst mere subjects – many, getting on for 40% of the world's population, of authoritarian and oppressive regimes.

Why is being able to vote so crucial, and how does it relate to all the other qualities and benefits that are commonly associated with citizenship? All but anarchists believe that we need some sort of stable political framework to regulate social and economic life, along with various political institutions – such as a bureaucracy, legal system and courts, a police force and army – to formulate and implement the necessary regulations. At a bare minimum, this framework will seek to preserve our bodies and property from physical harm by others, and provide clear and reasonably stable conditions for all the various forms of social interaction that most individuals find to some degree unavoidable – be it travelling on the roads, buying and selling goods and labour, or marriage and co-habitation. As we shall see, many people believe we need more than this bare minimum, but few doubt that in a society of any

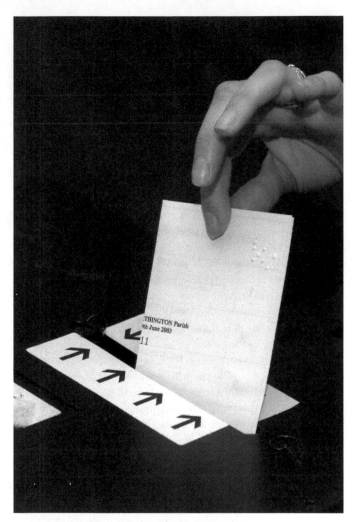

1. The crucial mark of citizenship is the right to vote

complexity we require at least these elements and that only a political community with properties similar to those we now associate with a state is going to provide them.

The social and moral dispositions that increasingly have come to be linked to citizenship, such as good neighbourliness, are certainly important supplements to any political framework, no matter how extensive. Rules and regulations cannot cover everything, and their being followed cannot depend on coercion alone. If people acted in a socially responsible way only because they feared being punished otherwise, it would be necessary to create a police state of totalitarian scope to preserve social order – a remedy potentially far worse than the disorder it would seek to prevent. But we cannot simply rely on people acting well either. It is not just that some people may take advantage of the goodness of others. Humans are also fallible creatures, possessing limited knowledge and reasoning power, and with the best will in the world are likely to err or disagree. Most complex problems raise a range of moral concerns, some of which may conflict, while the chain of cause and effect that produced them, and the likely consequences of any decisions we make to solve them, can all be very hard if not impossible to know for sure. Imagine if there was no highway code or traffic regulations and we had to coordinate with other drivers simply on the basis of us all possessing good judgement and behaving civilly and responsibly towards each other. Even if everyone acts conscientiously, there will be situations, such as blind corners or complicated interchanges, where we just lack the information to make competent judgements because it is impossible to second guess with any certainty what others might decide to do. Political regulation, say by installing traffic lights, in this and similar cases coordinates our interactions in ways that allow us to know where we stand with regard to others. In areas such as commerce, for example, that means we can enter into agreements and plan ahead with a degree of confidence.

Now any reasonably stable and efficient political framework, even one presided over by a ruthless tyrant, will provide us some of these benefits. For example, think of the increased uncertainty and insecurity suffered by many Iraqi citizens as a result of the lack of an effective political order following the toppling of Saddam Hussein. However, those possessing no great wealth, power, or influence – the vast majority of people in other words – will not be satisfied with just any framework. They will want one that applies to all – including the government – and treats everyone impartially and as equals, no matter how rich or important they may be. In particular, they will want its provisions to provide a just basis for all to enjoy the freedom to pursue their lives as they choose on equal terms with everyone else, and in so far as is compatible with their having a reasonable amount of personal security through the maintenance of an appropriate degree of social and political stability. And a necessary, if not always a sufficient, condition for ensuring the laws and policies of a political community possess these characteristics is that the country is a working electoral democracy and that citizens participate in making it so. Apart from anything else, political involvement helps citizens shape what this framework should look like. People are likely to disagree about what equality, freedom, and security involve and the best policies to support them in given circumstances. Democracy offers the potential for citizens to debate these issues on roughly equal terms and to come to some appreciation of each other's views and interests. It also promotes government that is responsive to their evolving concerns and changing conditions by giving politicians an incentive to rule in ways that reflect and advance not their own interests but those of most citizens.

The logic is simple, even if the practice often is not: if politicians consistently ignore citizens or prove incompetent, they will eventually lose office. Moreover, in a working democracy, where parties regularly alternate in power, a related incentive exists for citizens to listen to each other. Not only will very varied groups of citizens need to form alliances to build an electoral majority, often making compromises in the process, but also they will be aware that the composition of any future winning coalition is likely to shift and could exclude them. So the winners always have reason to be respectful of the needs and views of the losers.

As we shall see in Chapter 5, at its best democratic citizenship comes in this way to promote a degree of equity and reciprocity among citizens. For example, suppose the electorate contains 30% who want higher pensions, 40% wanting to lower taxes, 60% desiring more roads, 30% who want more trains, 60% supporting lower carbon emissions, 30% who oppose abortion, 60% who want better-funded hospitals, 30% who desire improved schools, 20% who want more houses built, and 35% who support fox hunting. I have made up these figures, but the distribution of support across a given range of political issues is not unlike that found in most democracies. Now, note how several policies are likely to prove incompatible with each other – spending more on one thing will mean less on another, improving hospitals may mean less spending on roads or schools, and so on. Note too how it is unlikely that any person or group will find themselves consistently in the majority or the minority on all issues – the minority who support hunting, say, is unlikely to overlap entirely with the minority who oppose abortion or the minority who want more houses. So I may be in a minority so far as my views on abortion are concerned and a majority when it comes to fox hunting, in a minority on schooling and a majority on road building, and so on. And each time I will be allied with a slightly different group of people.

Meanwhile, even when people broadly agree on an issue, they may disagree strongly about which policy best resolves it. So, a majority – say 60% – may agree we need to lower carbon emissions, but still disagree about how to do so – 30% may favour nuclear energy, 30% wind power, 20% measures for reducing the use of cars, 25% more green taxes, and so on. As a result, most people may in fact support very few policies that enjoy outright majority support – they will mainly be in different minorities alongside partly overlapping but often distinct groups of people. If a party wants to build a working majority, therefore, it will have to construct a coalition of minorities across a broad spectrum of issues and policies and arrange trade-offs between them. That makes it probable that most people will like some bits of the programmes of opposing parties and dislike other bits: a US voter might prefer the attitude towards abortion of most Democrats and the economic policies of most Republicans, say, and a UK voter the health policies of Labour and the EU policies of the Conservatives. They will cast their vote on the basis of a preponderance of things they like or dislike, appropriately weighted for what they regard as most important. Over time, as issues and attitudes change, party fortunes are likely to wax and wane and with them the extent to which the preferred policies of any individual voter coincide with a majority or a minority. 'One person, one vote' means that each person's preferences are treated in an equitable fashion, while the need for parties to address a range of people's views within their programmes forces citizens to practise a degree of mutual toleration and accommodation of each other's interests and concerns.

One can imagine circumstances in which a person could enjoy an equitable political framework without being a citizen. If someone is holidaying abroad in a stable democratic state, she will generally benefit from many of the advantages of its legal system and public services in much the same way as its citizens. The laws upholding most of her civil liberties will be identical, offering her similar rights to theirs against violent assault or fraud, say, and to a fair trial in the event that she is involved in such crimes. Likewise, she shall have many of the same obligations as a citizen and will have to obey those laws that concern her, such as speed limits if she is driving a car, paying sales tax on many goods, and so on. Most of the non-legally prescribed social duties that have become associated with citizenship will also apply. If she believes a socially responsible person should pick up litter, help old ladies across the road, avoid racist and sexist remarks, and buy only fair trade goods, then she has as much reason to abide by these norms abroad as at home. Indeed, similar considerations will lie behind her recognizing the value of following the laws of a foreign country, even though she has had no role in framing them. Likewise, to the extent the citizens of her host country are motivated by such considerations, they should act as civilly to visitors as they do towards their co-citizens. If she likes the country so much she decides to find a job and stay on for a while, then she will probably pay income tax and be protected by employment legislation and possibly even enjoy certain social benefits. Of course, in practice a number of contingent factors can put non-citizens at a disadvantage compared to many citizens in exercising their rights – especially if they are not fluent in the local language. But these sorts of disadvantages are not the direct result of not possessing the status of a citizen. After all, naturalized citizens might be in much the same position with regard to many of them. Nor need they prevent her, as a hardworking and polite individual who is solicitous towards others, from becoming a valued pillar of the local community, respected by her neighbours. Why then be bothered with being able to vote, do jury duty, and various other tasks many citizens find onerous – especially if she may never need any of the additional rights citizens enjoy?

There are two reasons why she ought to be concerned – both of which highlight why citizenship in the political sense is important. First, unlike citizens, she does not have an unqualified right to enter or remain in this country, and if she fell foul of the authorities could be refused entry or deported. As we shall see in subsequent chapters, this is a core right in an age when many people are stateless as a result of war or oppressive regimes in their countries of origin, or are driven by severe poverty to seek a better life elsewhere. But in a way it still begs the question of why she should want to become a citizen rather than simply a permanent resident. After all, most democratic countries acknowledge a humanitarian duty to help those in dire need and have established international agreements on asylum seekers to prevent individuals being turned away or returned to countries where their life would be in danger. Increasingly, there are also internationally recognized rights for long-term residents, or 'denizens' as they have come to be called. If she has lawfully entered the country and is a law-abiding individual, so there are no prospects of her being deported, then why not just enjoy living under its well-ordered regime? The second reason comes in here. For the qualities she likes about this country stem in large part from its democratic character. Even the quasi-citizenship status she has come to possess under international law is the product of international agreements that are promoted and reliably kept only by democratic states. And their being democracies depends in turn on at least a significant proportion of citizens within such states doing their duty and participating in the democratic process.

As I noted above, increasing numbers of citizens do not bother participating. They either feel it is pointless to do so or are happy to free-ride on the efforts of others. They are mistaken. It may well be that, as presently organized, democracy falls far short of the expectations citizens have of it, so that they feel their involvement has little or no effect. Yet that view is not so much an argument for abandoning democracy as for seeking to improve it. One need only compare life under any established democracy, imperfect though they all are, with that under any existing undemocratic regime to be aware that democracy makes a difference from which the majority of citizens draw tangible benefits. People lack self-respect, and possibly respect for others too, in a regime under which they do not have the possibility of expressing their views and being counted, no matter how benevolently and efficiently it is run. Rulers need no longer see the ruled as equals, as entitled to give an opinion and have their interests considered on the same terms as everyone else. And so they need not take them into account. Democratic citizenship changes the way power is exercised and the attitudes of citizens to each other. Because democracy gives us a share in ruling and in being ruled in the ways indicated above, citizenship allows us both to control our political leaders and to control ourselves and collaborate with our fellow citizens on a basis of equal concern and respect. By contrast, the permanent resident of my example is just a tolerated subject. She may express her views, but is not entitled to have them heard on an equal basis to citizens.

The components of citizenship: towards a definition

Citizenship, therefore, has an intrinsic link to democratic politics. It involves membership of an exclusive club – those who take the key decisions about the collective life of a given political community. And the character of that community in many ways reflects what people make it. In particular, their participation or lack of it plays an important role in determining how far, and in what ways, it treats people as equals. Three linked components of citizenship emerge from this analysis – membership of a democratic political community, the collective benefits and rights associated with membership, and participation in the community's political, economic, and social processes – all of which combine in different ways to establish a condition of civic equality.

The first component, membership or belonging, concerns who is a citizen. In the past, many have been excluded from within as well as outside the political community. Internal exclusions have included those designated as natural inferiors on racial, gender, or other grounds; or as unqualified due to a lack of property or education; or as disqualified through having committed a crime or become jobless, homeless, or mentally ill. So, in most established democracies women obtained the vote long after the achievement of universal male suffrage, before which many workers were excluded, while prisoners often lose their right to vote, as does – by default – anyone who does not have a fixed address. Many of these internal grounds for exclusion have been dropped as baseless, though others remain live issues, as does the unequal effectiveness of the right to vote among different groups. However, much recent attention has concentrated on the external exclusions of asylum seekers and immigrants. Here, too, there have been changes towards more inclusive policies at both the domestic and international levels, though significant exclusionary measures persist or have recently been introduced. Yet, the current high levels of international migration, though not unprecedented, have been sufficiently intense and prolonged and of such global scope as to have forced a major rethink of the criteria for citizenship.

As we shall see in later chapters, none of these criteria proves straightforward. Citizenship implies the capacity to participate in both the political and the socio-economic life of the community. Yet, the nature of that participation and the capabilities it calls for have varied over time and remain matters of debate. Citizens must also be willing to see themselves as in some sense belonging to the particular state in which they reside. At the very least, they must recognize it as a centre of power entitled to regulate their behaviour, demand taxes, and so on, in return for providing them with various public goods. How far they must also identify with their fellow citizens is a different matter. A working democracy certainly requires some elements of a common civic culture: notably, broad acceptance of the legitimacy of the prevailing rules of politics and probably a common language or languages for political debate. A degree of trust and solidarity among citizens also proves important if all are to collaborate in producing the collective benefits of citizenship, rather than some attempting to free-ride on the efforts of others. The extent to which such qualities depend on citizens possessing a shared identity is a more contested, yet crucial, issue as societies become increasingly multicultural.

The second component, rights, has often been seen as the defining criterion of citizenship. Contemporary political philosophers have adopted two main approaches to identifying these rights. A first approach seeks to identify those rights that citizens ought to acknowledge if they are to treat each other as free individuals worthy of equal concern and respect. A second approach tries, more modestly, simply to identify the rights that are necessary if citizens are to participate in democratic decision-making on free and equal terms. Both approaches prove problematic. Even if most committed democrats broadly accept the legitimacy of one or other of these accounts of citizens' rights as being implicit in the very idea of democracy, they come to very different conclusions about the precise rights either approach might generate. These differences largely reflect the various ideological and other divisions that form the mainstay of contemporary democratic politics. So neo-liberals are likely to regard the free market as sufficient to show individuals equality of concern and respect with regard to their social and economic rights, whereas a social democrat is more likely to wish to see a publicly supported health service and social security system too. Similarly, some people might advocate a given system of proportional representation as necessary to guarantee a citizen's equal right to vote, others view the plurality first past the post system as sufficient or even, in some respects, superior. As a result of these disagreements, the rights of citizenship have to be seen, somewhat paradoxically perhaps, as subject to the decisions of citizens themselves.

That paradox seems less acute, though, once we also note that making rights the primary consideration is in various respects too reductive. We tend to see rights as individual entitlements – they are claims individuals can make against others, including governments, to certain standards of decency in the way they are treated. However, though rights attach to individuals, they have an important collective dimension that the link with citizenship serves to highlight. What does the work in any account of rights is not the appeal to rights as such but to the arguments for why people have those rights. Most of these arguments have two elements. First, they appeal to certain goods as being important for human beings to be able to lead a life that reflects their own free choices and effort – usually the absence of coercion by others and certain material preconditions for agency, such as food, shelter, and health. Second, and most importantly from our point of view, they imply that social relations should be so organized that we secure these rights on an equal basis for all. Rights are collective goods in two important senses, therefore. On the one hand, they assume that we all share an interest in certain goods as important for us to be able to shape our own lives. On the other hand, these rights can only be provided by people accepting certain civic duties that ensure they are respected, including cooperating to set up appropriate collective arrangements. For example, if we take personal security as an uncontentious shared human good, then a right to this good can only be protected if all refrain from illegitimate interference with others and collaborate to establish a legal system and police force that upholds that right in a fair manner that treats all as equals. In other words, we return to the arguments establishing the priority of political citizenship canvassed earlier. For rights depend on the existence of some form of political community in which citizens seek fair terms of association to secure those goods necessary for them to pursue their lives on equal terms with others. Hence, the association of rights with the rights of democratic citizens, with citizenship itself forming the right of rights because it is the 'right to have rights' – the capacity to institutionalize the rights of citizens in an appropriately egalitarian way.

The third component, participation, comes in here. Calling citizenship the 'right to have rights' indicates how access to numerous rights depends on membership of a political community. However, many human rights activists have criticized the exclusive character of citizenship for this very reason, maintaining that rights ought to be available to all on an equal basis regardless of where you are born or happen to live. As a result, they have sometimes argued against any limits on access to citizenship. Rights should transcend the boundaries of any political community and not depend on either membership or participation. Though there is much justice in these criticisms, they are deficient in three main respects.

First, the citizens of well-run democracies enjoy a level and range of entitlements that extend beyond what most people would characterize as human rights – that is, rights that we are entitled to simply on humanitarian grounds. Of course, it could be argued with some justification that many of these countries have benefited from the indirect or direct exploitation of poorer, often non-democratic, states and various related human rights abuses, such as selling arms to their authoritarian rulers. Rectifying these abuses, though, would still allow for significant differentials in wealth between countries. For, second, rights also result from the positive activities of citizens themselves and their contributions to the collective goods of their political community. In this respect, citizenship forms the 'right to have rights' in placing in citizens' own hands the ability to decide which rights they will provide for and how. Some countries might choose to have high taxes and generous public health, education, and social security schemes, say, others to have lower taxes and less generous public provision of these goods, or more spending on culture or on police and the armed forces. Finally, none of the above rules out recognizing the 'right to have rights' as a human right that creates an obligation on the part of existing democratic states to aid rather than hinder democratization processes in non-democratic states, to give succour to asylum seekers and to have equitable and non-discriminatory naturalization procedures for migrant workers willing to commit to the duties of citizenship in their adopted countries.

So membership, rights, and participation go together. It is through being a member of a political community and participating on equal terms in the framing of its collective life that we enjoy rights to pursue our individual lives on fair terms with others. If we put these three components together, we come up with the following definition of citizenship:

> Citizenship is a condition of civic equality. It consists of membership of a political community where all citizens can determine the terms of social cooperation on an equal basis. This status not only secures equal rights to the enjoyment of the collective goods provided by the political association but also involves equal duties to promote and sustain them – including the good of democratic citizenship itself.

The paradox and dilemma of citizenship

Earlier I suggested that citizenship involves a paradox encapsulated in viewing it as the 'right to have rights'. That paradox consists in our rights as citizens being dependent on our exercising our basic citizenship right to political participation in cooperation with our fellow citizens. For our rights derive from the collective policies we decide upon to resolve common problems, such as providing for personal security with a police force and legal system. Moreover, once in place, these policies will only operate if we continue to cooperate to maintain them through paying taxes and respecting the rights of others that follow from them. So rights involve duties – not least the duty to exercise the political rights to participate on which all our other rights depend. This paradox gives rise in its turn to a dilemma that can affect much cooperative behaviour. Namely, that we will be tempted to shirk our civic duties if we feel we can enjoy the collective goods and the rights they provide by relying on others to do their bit rather than exerting ourselves. And the more citizens act in this way, the less they will trust their fellow citizens to collaborate with them. Collective arrangements will seem increasingly unreliable, prompting people to abandon citizenship for other, more individualistic, ways of securing their interests.

This dilemma proves particularly acute if the good in question has the qualities associated with what is technically known as a 'public good' – that is a good, such as street lighting, from which nobody can be excluded from the benefits, regardless of whether they contributed to supporting it or not. In such cases, a temptation will exist for individuals to 'free-ride' on the efforts of others. So, if the neighbours either side of my house pay for a street light, they will not be able to stop me benefiting from it even if I choose not to help them with the costs. In many respects, democracy operates as a public good of this kind and so likewise confronts the quandary of free-riding. The cost of becoming informed and casting your vote is immediate and felt directly by each individual, while the benefits are far less tangible and individualized, as are the disadvantages of not voting. You will gain from living in a democracy whether you vote or not, while any individual vote contributes very little to sustaining democratic institutions. And the shortcomings of democracy – the policies and politicians people dislike – tend to be more evident than its virtues, which are diffuse, and in newly democratized countries, often long term. As a result, the temptation to free-ride is great.

In fact, political scientists used to be puzzled why citizens bothered to vote at all – it seemed irrational. Given the very small likelihood any one person's vote will make a difference to the election result, it hardly seems worth the effort. Even the fear that democracy may collapse should have little effect on this self-centred reasoning. As an individual, it still pays the free-rider to rely on the efforts of others. After all, if others fail to do their part, there will be little point in the free-rider doing so. In the past, it seems that citizens simply were not so narrowly instrumental in their reasoning. They appear to have valued the opportunity of expressing their views along with others. The growing fear, symbolized by the decline in voting, is that such civic-mindedness has lessened, with citizens becoming more self-interested and calculating in their attitudes not just to political participation but also to the collective goods political authorities exist to provide. They have also felt that their fellow citizens and politicians are likewise concerned only with their own interests. American national election studies, for example, reveal that over the past 40 years the majority of US citizens have come to feel that government benefits a few major interests rather than those of everyone, although the percentage has fluctuated between lows of 24% and 19% in 1974 and 1994 respectively believing it benefited all, to highs of 39% and 40% in 1984 and 2004. Likewise, a British opinion poll of 1996 revealed that a staggering 88% of respondents believed Members of Parliament served interests other than their constituents' or the country's – with 56% contending they simply served their own agenda.

This change in people's attitudes and perceptions presents a major challenge to the practice and purpose of citizenship. Most of the collective goods that citizens collaborate to support and on which their rights depend are subject to the public goods dilemma described above. Like voting, the cost of the tax I pay to support the police, roads, schools, and hospitals will seem somehow more direct and personal than the benefits I derive from these goods, and a mere drop in the ocean compared to the billions needed to pay for them. Like democracy, these goods also tend to be available to all citizens regardless of how much they pay or, indeed, whether they have paid at all. True, these goods do not have the precise quality of public goods – some degree of exclusion is possible. However, it would be both inefficient and potentially create great injustices to do so. Moreover, in numerous indirect ways we all do benefit from a good transport system, a healthy and well-educated population, and from others as well as ourselves enjoying personal security. That said, people will always be naturally inclined to wonder whether they are getting value for money or are contributing more than their fair share. Such concerns are likely to be particularly acute if people feel little sense of solidarity with each other or believe others to be untrustworthy, especially when it comes to the sort of redistributive measures needed to support most social rights. Consequently, the inducements to adopt independent, non-cooperative behaviour for more apparently secure, short-term advantages will be great – even if, as will often be the case, such decisions have the perverse long-term effect of proving more costly or less beneficial not just for the community as a whole but even for most of the defecting individuals.

This tendency has been apparent in the trend within developed democracies for wealthier citizens to contract into private arrangements in ever more areas, from education and health to pensions and even personal security, often detracting from public provision in the process. So, people have opted to send their children to private schools, taken out private health insurance, employed private security firms to police their gated neighbourhoods, and sought to pay less in taxation for public schemes. But the net result has often been that the cost of education, health, and policing has risen because a proliferation of different private insurance schemes proves less efficient, while the depleted public provision brings in its wake a number of costly social problems – a less well-educated and healthy workforce, more crime, and so on.

Governments have responded to this development in four main ways. First, they have partly marketized some of these services, in form if not always in substance. One consequence of it being either technically impossible or morally unjust to exclude people from the benefits of 'public goods' is that standard market incentives do not operate. Companies have no reason to compete for customers by offering lower prices or better products if they cannot restrict enjoyment of a good to those who have paid them for it. Governments have tried to overcome this problem by getting companies periodically to compete for the contract to supply a given public service and by trying to guarantee citizens certain rights as customers. In so doing, they have stressed the state's role as a regulator rather than necessarily as a provider of services. The aim is to guarantee that given standards and levels of provision are met, regardless of whether a public or a private contractor actually offers the service concerned. In this way,

2. The rich have increasingly withdrawn from the collective provision of public goods

governments have tried to reassure citizens that as much attention will be paid to getting value for money and meeting their requirements as would be the case if they were buying the service on their own account. Their second response has complemented this strategy by stressing the responsibilities of citizens – especially of those who are net recipients of state support. For example, a number of states have obliged recipients of social security benefits to be available for and actively to seek work, engage in retraining, and possibly to do various forms of community service. By such measures, they have tried to reassure net contributors to the system that all are pulling their weight and so retain their allegiance to collective arrangements. Third, they have adopted an increasingly marketized approach to the very practice of electoral politics. They have conducted consumer research as to citizens' preferences and attempted to woo them through branding and advertising. Finally, they have attempted to overcome cynicism about using state power to support the public interest by depoliticizing standard-setting and the regulation of the economic and political markets alike to supposedly impartial bodies immune from self-interest, such as independent banks and the courts.

These policies have had mixed results. By and large, they have been most successful for those services that can be most fully marketized, such as some of the former public utilities like gas, electricity, and telephones, and where there are reasonably clear, technical criteria for what a good service should be and how it might be obtained. For other goods – particularly those where the imperatives for public provision are as much moral as economic, and defection into private arrangements is comparatively easy, such as health care or education – a partial withdrawal from, and a resulting attenuation of, public services has occurred in many advanced democratic states.

Meanwhile, disillusion about politics has grown. Citizens have increasingly felt politicians will do anything for their vote and once in power employ it selfishly and ineptly. Civic solidarity has decreased accordingly as inequalities have grown between social groups. While the better educated and wealthier sections of society have pushed governments and politicians to do less and less, the poorer sections, who find it harder to organize in any case, have increasingly withdrawn from politics altogether. The problem seems to be two-fold. On the one hand, citizens have adopted a more consumer-orientated and critical view of democratic politics. They have taken a more self-interested stance, assuming that others, their fellow citizens, politicians, and those in the public sector more generally, do so too. On the other hand, politicians have likewise treated citizens more like consumers and both marketized the public sector where possible and acted themselves rather like the heads of rival firms. Commentators differ as to which came first, but most accept these two developments have fuelled each other, producing increasing disillusionment with democratic politics. Instead of being viewed as a means of bringing citizens together in pursuit of those public interests from which they collectively benefit, politics has come to be seen as but an inefficient mechanism for individuals to pursue their private interests.

Globalization has been widely perceived as further promoting both these sources of political disaffection. That many public goods, from security against crime to monetary stability, can only be obtained through international mechanisms has added to civic disaffection and the belief in the shortcomings of political measures. International organizations are inevitably much more distant from the citizens they serve. Size matters, and it is much harder to feel solidarity with very large and highly diverse groups with whom one has few, if any, shared cultural or other references and hardly any direct interaction. As a result, short-term individualized behaviour is much more likely. Put simply, cheating on strangers is easier than with people you meet every day and will continue to interact with into the foreseeable future. The more complex and globalized societies are, the more we all become strangers to each other. It also becomes much harder to influence or hold politicians to account. Your vote is one in millions rather than thousands, and it is more difficult to combine with others in groups sharing one's interests and concerns that are of sufficient size to influence those with power. Again, markets and weak forms of depoliticized regulation have come to be seen as more competent and impartial than collective political solutions.

The European Union (EU), the world's most developed international organization, reflects these dilemmas and responses well. Despite having elections and a parliament, European politicians are both little trusted and scarcely known, while electoral turnout is far below that for national elections of the member states and likewise on the decline. By and large, citizens have remained tied to their national or subnational allegiances and mainly, and increasingly, view the EU in narrowly self-interested terms as either beneficial or not to their country or economic group. European political parties exist largely as voting blocks of national parties within the European Parliament, while the vast majority of trans-European civil society organizations are small, Brussels-based lobby groups, with few if any members and invariably reliant on the EU for funding. Meanwhile, the EU has increasingly sought to legitimize itself through non-political means, notably appeals to supposed 'European' values, such as rights, on the one side, and as an efficient, effective, equitable, and depoliticized economic regulator, on the other.

Developments in the EU mirror what has happened in most established democratic states, including those outside Europe, such as the United States, Canada, Australia, and New Zealand. Worries about a decline in civic attitudes and voting has produced a concern with the collapse of 'social capital' – the habit of collaborating and joining with others, summed up in Robert Putnam's observation that Americans no longer go ten pin bowling in teams but more and more 'bowl alone'. Increased immigration and growing multiculturalism are also feared to have reduced community feeling based on a common culture. As a result, governments have sought to inculcate a sense of national and civic belonging through an enhanced emphasis on citizenship education in schools and for immigrants seeking to naturalize. This teaching has usually emphasized national culture broadly conceived rather than political culture in the narrower, democratic sense. Likewise, they have increasingly claimed to have depoliticized important decisions – handing the setting of interest rates over to national banks, emphasizing deference to constitutional courts in matters of protecting rights, and using independent regulators to oversee not only the former public utilities, such as gas and water, but also many other social and economic areas, such as sentencing policy. In these ways, they have tried to separate membership and rights from participation.

Yet, it is dubious that such attempts will be effective. Political communities and rights alike are constructed and sustained by the activities of citizens. People feel bound to each other and by the law only if they regard themselves as involved in shaping their relationships with each other and the state through their ability to influence the rules, policies, and politicians that govern social life. Indeed, they have good grounds for believing they are not civic equals without that capacity. So appeals to political community or rights will not of themselves create citizenship because they are the products of citizenly action through political participation. People will not feel any sense of ownership over them. The three components of citizenship stand and fall together.

Both social and economic changes and the political responses to them are challenging the very possibility of citizenship, therefore. This book explores these challenges further. We start in Chapter 2 by sketching the historical development of citizenship from the city states of ancient Greece to the nation states of the 20th century. In many respects, this history provides the resources for current thinking about citizenship. Chapters 3, 4, and 5 then examine membership, rights, and participation in turn, noting how each is being transformed in ways that are changing the character and perhaps the feasibility of citizenship today. Throughout I stress the need to see these three elements as a package, with political participation offering the indispensable glue holding them together.

Chapter 2
Theories of citizenship and their history

Theories of citizenship fall into two types: normative theories that attempt to set out the rights and duties a citizen ideally ought to have, and empirical theories that seek to describe and explain how citizens came to possess those rights and duties that they actually have. In different but related ways, both types of theory appeal to history.

Normative theories look to history to explore the ideal of the good citizen. Past accounts of citizenship have inevitably shaped how we think about what it is to be a citizen. They provide a sort of scrapbook of ideas about the attributes and advantages of citizenship: who is a citizen, the kind of contribution the state and other citizens can expect of him or her and under which circumstances, and what he or she can expect of them and when. Accordingly, contemporary normative theories of citizenship tend to elaborate upon and test themselves against older views. They point out the logical inconsistencies of past theories, drop certain elements on the grounds of their outdatedness or undesirability, and embellish or add others as more appropriate to present conditions in order to come up with what they believe is the best possible account of citizenship today. For example, military service was an integral part of older views of citizenship, but has gradually been dropped in more recent accounts. But some of the reasons that made a willingness to die for one's country an important part of past theories of the good citizen, such as patriotism and a strong identification with one's co-nationals, still figure as desirable qualities of citizenship in many later accounts, as we shall see in Chapter 3.

By contrast, empirical theories explore the social, economic, and political processes that have fashioned the emergence of citizenship in different times and places, and the ways this status has been granted to different groups of people. These theories seek to understand how and why citizenship arose in given circumstances and took the forms it did. However, it would be wrong to regard these accounts as purely explanatory. Implicitly or explicitly, they are invariably motivated by a particular normative ideal and focus on identifying the ways certain normative possibilities were foreclosed or opened up. Indeed, normative theories themselves play an independent role within any explanatory theory of citizenship by legitimizing and shaping the demands and actions of the various social and political actors who create citizenship. So, people in ancient Greece and Rome had very different views of the ideal of citizenship to ours and these provided a justification for the way these societies were organized. But elaborations of these same ideals have also inspired many later thinkers and activists – including some today – to militate for changes to the way citizenship is practised or defined within their own very different societies.

This chapter cannot do justice to the full range of theories of either type. Instead, I am going to concentrate on those theories that feature most prominently in contemporary debates. I shall start by looking at two historically important normative theories, their subsequent elaboration, and their modern variants. As we shall see, the dominant 'models' of citizenship are very much rooted in ancient Greece and Rome, with these two 'classic' accounts orientating much later thinking on the topic. I shall then turn to the most influential empirical theories. These concern the development of democratic citizenship within the nation states of

Western Europe. Yet these theories have often had a normative purpose of their own: namely, to see the democratic, welfare states that arose after the Second World War as partial realizations and syntheses of various aspects of the two dominant normative models of citizenship. The key debate, explored in much of the rest of the book, is whether these normative models remain relevant as spurs to further developing the scope and substance of citizenship or reflect unattainable and possibly undesirable aspirations that we would do well to renounce.

Two models of citizenship

In an important essay, the historian of ideas J. G. A. Pocock observed how the Greek and Roman characterizations of citizenship offer the classical models not only because they belong to the 'classical' period of history but also in setting the terms of much later debate on the subject. The so-called Greek model of citizenship is drawn principally from the writings of Aristotle and what we know of the political system in Athens and, to a lesser extent, Sparta in the 5th and 4th centuries BC.

The key feature of this view was the equality of citizens as rulers or makers of the law. Along with the writings of defenders and analysts of the Roman republic of c. 510–27 BC, the Greek model and its Roman republican variants have inspired those theories of citizenship that stress political participation as its defining element. By contrast, Pocock identifies what he calls the Roman model of citizenship with imperial Rome. The key feature of this view of citizenship was equality under the law. As such, it could be extended to all subjects of the Roman Empire. This account inspires those later theories of citizenship that see equality of legal status as its main element.

Clearly, to construct a history of the idea of citizenship around these two models is overly schematic. However, it remains true that later thinkers frequently refer back to them, be it to bemoan

3. Aristotle, the theorist of the Greek model of citizenship

their passing, refine and update them, or to denounce them and advocate the need to begin afresh. In particular, much contemporary thinking and theorizing about citizenship can be roughly characterized as an attempt to elaborate on one or other of them and possibly overcome the tensions between them. So, even if dubious as history, it is a justifiable exercise in historiography – or the tracing of how certain people have thought about the past – to look at the citizenship tradition in Western political thought through the lens of these two views.

Citizenship as equal participation: ancient Greece and the Roman republic

As I noted, the Greek model is largely inspired by the writings of Aristotle, particularly his account of citizenship in *The Politics*, written some time between 335 and 323 BC. Aristotle regarded human beings as 'political animals' because it is in our nature to live in political communities – indeed, he contended, only within a *polis*, or city state, could human potential be fully realized. However, people played the roles appropriate to what Aristotle believed was their natural station in life, with only some qualifying as *polites*, or citizens. Though neither the qualifications Aristotle deemed appropriate for membership of this select group nor the duties he expected of them are regarded as entirely suitable today, they have cast a long shadow over the history of citizenship and their fundamental rationale still underlies much contemporary thinking.

To be a citizen it was necessary to be a male aged 20 or over, of known genealogy as being born to an Athenian citizen family, to be a patriarch of a household, a warrior – possessing the arms and ability to fight – and a master of the labour of others, notably slaves. So gender, race, and class defined citizenship, and as we shall see in the next chapter, many of the main contemporary debates turn on how far they continue to do so. As a result, large numbers were excluded: women (though married Athenian women were citizens for genealogical purposes); children; immigrants, or 'metics' – including those whose families had been settled in Athens for several generations (although they were legally free, liable to taxation, and had military duties); and above all, slaves. It is reckoned that the number of citizens in Athens fluctuated between 30,000 and 50,000, while the number of slaves was of the order of 80,000 to 100,000. Therefore, citizenship was enjoyed by a minority, though a substantial one. Yet, this was inevitable given the high expectations of citizens. For their capacity to perform their not inconsiderable citizenly duties rested on their everyday needs being looked after by the majority of the population, particularly women and slaves.

Aristotle described as citizens 'all who share in the civic life of ruling and being ruled in turn'. Though he acknowledged that what this entailed differed between polities and even between different categories of citizen within the same city state, he considered it to involve at some level 'the right of sharing in deliberative and judicial office'. In Athens this meant at a minimum participating in the Assembly, which met at least 40 times a year and required a quorum of 6,000 citizens for plenary sessions, and, for citizens aged over 30, doing jury service – again, a frequent responsibility given that juries numbered 201 or more, and on some occasions over 501. All the major issues came before the Assembly – declarations of war and the concluding of peace, the forming of alliances, public order, and finance and taxation. In addition, there were some 140 local territorial units of government, or *demes*, and these constructed their own *agorae*, or assembly points for public discussion of local affairs and decrees. Unlike involvement in the assemblies, jury service was at least paid. However, jurors were chosen by lot from among those who presented themselves to discourage both its becoming a regular income and jury packing.

Meanwhile, many citizens could not avoid also holding public office at some period. With the exception of generals, who were elected by the Assembly and could serve multiple terms for as long as they were successful, public offices were chosen by lot and usually held for one or a maximum of two years. The aim of these devices was to increase the likelihood that all would have an equal chance of exercising political power, although the short terms of office and the checks operated by the different bodies on each other meant this power was severely circumscribed. Citizens were organized into 10 'tribes' based on residence, with each selecting 50 councillors chosen by lot from among candidates elected by the *demes* to sit in the Council of 500 for a year. They all served for a tenth of their term on the Committee of 50, which proposed legislation, and for one day as the president of the Committee. Day-to-day administration was in the hands of some 1,200 'magistrates', chosen annually by lot from those who stood for office, with the period of service restricted to two terms. Although all public offices were paid, selection by lottery and short terms meant there could be no career politicians. Yet, citizenship itself, if one adds military service and participation in local affairs, was a fairly full occupation.

Athens was unusual among Greek city states in being so democratic. Indeed, Aristotle, who periodically resided in Athens but was not born there and so not an Athenian citizen, expressed a personal preference for systems that mixed democracy with aristocratic and monarchical elements. However, even in those systems that did so, citizenship remained fairly onerous. For example, like his mentor Plato, Aristotle had a certain, if more mooted, admiration for the much more austere citizenship code of Sparta. By contrast to Athens, where the arts, philosophy, and the cultivation of leisure were much admired, Sparta emphasized military service above all else. Children were separated from their families aged 7 and subjected to a rigorous training, and thereafter were attached to a 'mess'. Given that they still had to attend the Assembly, Spartan citizens became even more permanent public servants than their Athenian counterparts. In fact, it was precisely their limited opportunities to develop private interests that Plato in particular so admired.

Aristotle acknowledged that such forms of citizenship were likely to be possible only in fairly small states. That was important not just so everyone could have a turn at ruling and to keep the tasks of government sufficiently simple as to be manageable without a professional bureaucracy or political class, but also because it was only in smaller settings that the requisite civic virtues were likely to be fostered. Although the Athenians probably invented the idea of taking a vote to settle disagreements, unanimity was the ideal, and it appears likely that most issues were settled by consensus – if need be, following extended debate. Aristotle surmised that such concord, or *homonoia*, depended on a form of civic friendship among citizens that was likely to proceed only from living together in a tightly knit community. Citizens must know each other, share values, and have common interests. Only then are they likely to be able to agree on which qualities are best for given offices and select the right people for them, harmoniously resolve disputed rights, and adopt collective policies unanimously. Even so, agreement rested on citizens possessing a sense of justice, being temperate by exercising self-control and avoiding extremes, having a capacity for prudent judgement, being motivated by patriotism, so they put the public good above private advantage, and being courageous before danger, especially military threats. In sum, a citizen must not belong 'just to himself' but also to 'the *polis*'.

Though in the Greek model citizenship was the privilege of a minority, it provided a considerable degree of popular control over government. Of course, we know that the Assembly and Council tended to be dominated by the high born and wealthy. It is also true that Aristotle's ideal of concord was often far from the reality, at least in Athens. There were persistent tensions between different classes and factions. Disagreements there were often bitter and personal, ending with the physical removal of opponents through ostracism or even their execution on trumped-up charges of treason. Nonetheless, in a very real sense those people who qualified as citizens did rule, thereby giving us the word 'democracy', from the Greek *demokratia*, or people (*demos*) rule (*kratos*).

Unsurprisingly, Greek citizenship has appeared to many later thinkers as the epitome of a true condition of political equality, in which citizens have equal political powers and so must treat each other with equal concern and respect. They have viewed the trend towards delegating political tasks to a professional class of politicians and public administrators with foreboding, as presaging a loss of political freedom and equality, and lamented the – in their opinion – short-sighted tendency for ever more citizens to desert public service to pursue personal concerns. By contrast, critics of this model of citizenship argue that it was not so much an ideal as hopelessly idealized. In reality, it was doubly oppressive. On the one hand, it rested on the oppression of slaves, women, and other non-citizens. On the other hand, it was oppressive of citizens in demanding they sacrifice their private interests to the service of the state. As we saw, the two forms of oppression were linked: citizens could only dedicate themselves to public life because their private lives were serviced by others. Both have also been the mark of totalitarian regimes. The latter too have typically treated non-citizens as less than fully human and have demanded not just allegiance but also the total identification of citizens with the state, regarding all dissent as indicative of self-interest rather than an alternative point of view or valid concern. As well as being repressive, such systems tend to be highly inefficient – not least in diverting all talent away from the private sphere of the economy on which the wealth of a society rests. Contrary to what was intended, making the public sphere the main avenue of personal advancement can lead to corruption and the abuse of public power for private again.

Both republican and imperial Rome offer important contrasts in these respects. The Roman republican model of citizenship is sometimes collapsed into the Greek model. But while there are some similarities, there are also striking differences. Though classes existed in Greek society, including among those who qualified as citizens, the ideal of citizenship became classless with the aspiration to 'concord', a product of putting class and other private interests to one side. By contrast, the Roman republic was born of class discord and the struggle of the plebeians to obtain rights against the patricians. The key event in this early history was the 'secession' of the plebeians to the Aventine Hill in 494 BC, where they swore an oath of mutual support to get the patricians to appoint officials who would look after their interests, a move that led to the creation of Tribunes of the People, elected by a new Plebeian Council, who possessed the power to veto the acts of other magistrates, including each other. The Plebeian Council also dealt with civil litigation, though this function fell with the creation of permanent courts, and most importantly had the power to pass laws (*plebiscita*). Initially, these laws applied only to the common people, but ultimately encompassed all classes. Three other popularly elected assemblies existed: one based on family clan groupings, one elected by serving soldiers based on their legionary units, or centuries, and a third based on tribal divisions. However, these exercised judicial rather than legislative powers.

Despite being able to vote for and sit on all these bodies, as well as being eligible to become Tribunes and magistrates, Roman citizens never possessed anything like the political influence of their Athenian counterparts. True power rested with the Senate. While entry to the Senate ceased to depend on rank around 400 BC, being composed instead of popularly elected magistrates, it was dominated by the patricians – especially among the higher magistracy, particularly the Consuls who formed the executive. The slogan *Senatus Populusque Romanus* ('The Senate and the Roman People', frequently abbreviated to SPQR) suggested a partnership between the Senate and the people within the popular assemblies. In reality, Senate and people were always in tension, with the influence of the plebeians waxing and waning depending on their importance as support for different factions among the patricians. As the historians of the Roman republic and, drawing on them, Machiavelli and other later neo-Roman republican theorists appreciated, this ongoing class conflict gave politics and citizenship a much more instrumental character than the Greek ideal of disinterested service to the public good. Although Roman republicans such as Cicero characterized civic virtue in similar terms to the Greeks, as selfless devotion to public duty, and warned against the pursuit of riches as a source of corruption in and out of office, few were willing to emulate the modest farming lifestyle of Cincinnatus, the model Roman republican hero, who according to legend abandoned his plough to save the republic and returned to it once the task was done. The Roman patriciate was fabulously wealthy.

4. Machiavelli, the theorist of Roman republican citizenship

In Machiavelli's eyes, the true lesson of the Roman experience was that the selfish interests of the aristocracy and the people could only be restrained if each could counter the other. The republic institutionalized such mutual restraint by ensuring no person or institution could exercise power except in combination with at least one other person or institution, so both could check and balance each other. Accordingly, there were two Consuls, each able to veto the other's decisions, ten Tribunes with similar countervailing powers, and so on, with none able to hold office for more than a year. The need to divide power in this way was elaborated by later republican theorists. It was a key feature of the city states of Renaissance Italy, especially Florence and Venice, which inspired Machiavelli's writings on the subject, and informed the constitutional debates of the English Civil War of the 17th century and the political arrangements of the Dutch republic into the 18th century. In the work of the American Federalists, especially Madison, the division of powers became a central element of the US Constitution. Underlying this account was a distinctively realist view of citizenship, which would be more easily adaptable to modern democratic politics than the Greek view. Instead of viewing the private interest and the public interest as diametrically opposed, so that all elements of the first had to be removed from politics, the public interest emerged from the clash and balancing of private interests. Consequently, citizens had self-interested reasons to participate because they could only ensure their concerns figured in any collective decisions so long as they took part and were counted. Indeed, when we turn to the descriptive theories, we shall see how modern citizenship has largely developed from the struggles of different groups to have their interests addressed on an equal basis to others.

Citizenship as equal legal status: from imperial Rome to human rights

As the Roman republic became overlaid by the Empire, the link between citizenship and private interests underwent a dramatic change. Eligibility for Roman citizenship was at first similar to the criteria for Greek citizenship – citizens had to be native free men who were the legitimate sons of other native free men. As Rome expanded – initially within Italy, then over the rest of Europe, and finally into Africa and Asia – two important innovations came about. First, the populations of conquered territories were given a version of Roman citizenship while being allowed to retain their own forms of government, including whatever citizenship status they offered. Second, the version of Roman citizenship given was of a legal rather than a political kind – *'civitas sine suffragio'*, or 'citizenship without the vote'. So, the Empire allowed dual citizenship, though it reduced Roman citizenship to a legal status. As a result, the legal and political communities pulled apart. The scope of law went beyond political borders and did not need to be co-extensive with a given territorial unit. To cite the famous case of St Paul – on arrest in Palestine, he proudly declared himself 'a Jew of Tarsus, a city in Cilicia, a citizen of no mean city'. But not being in Tarsus, it was his additional status as a Roman citizen that allowed him to claim rights against arbitrary punishment, thereby escaping a whipping, and to ask for trial in Rome.

According to the Aristotelian ideal, political citizenship had depended on being freed from the burdens of economic and social life – both in order to participate and to ensure that public rather than private interests were the object of concern. By contrast, legal citizenship has private interests and their protection at its heart. Within Roman law, legal status belonged to the owners of property and, by extension, their possessions. Since these included slaves, a free person was one who owned himself. So conceived, as in many respects it remains to this day, law was about how we could use ourselves and our things and those of others, and the use they may make of us and our things. As the example of St Paul shows, the resulting privileges and immunities, including the right to sue and be sued in given courts, were far from trivial. However, that the rule of law can be detached from the rule of persons, in that those subject to it do not have to be involved in either its making or its administration, creates disadvantages as well as advantages.

The advantage is that the legal community can, as we saw, encompass a number of political communities and hold their rulers and officers to account, thereby limiting their discretion to act against the law. Law can be universal in scope and extent, enabling millions of dispersed individuals to pursue their private interests by engaging and exchanging with each other across space and, through such legal acts as bequests, through time, without any direct contact. The disadvantage lies in these same citizens becoming the imperial subjects of the law's empire, who are ruled by it rather than ruling themselves. Yet the rule of law is only ever rule through law by some person or persons. Law can have many sources and enforcers, and different laws and legal systems will apply to different groups of persons and have differing costs and benefits for each of them. If law's empire depends on an emperor, then the danger is that law becomes a means for imperial rule rather than rule of and for the public.

Of course, a tradition quickly emerged that identified the source of law beyond the will of any human agent or agency – seeking it instead in nature, God's will or reason. These arguments offer different intellectual constructions of what they claim to be the fundamental law of all human associations. Such law supposedly operates as a superior or higher law, which binds all political rulers – be it an absolute monarch or the people themselves – and trumps whatever laws they may pass. These depictions of fundamental law have proved tremendously influential in international law, especially human rights law, and lie behind many arguments for domestic constitutions. They inform many of the contemporary rights-based conceptions of citizenship explored in Chapter 4. However, such accounts always come up against the self-same problem that, as with ordinary law, only persons can interpret and implement higher or fundamental law – that, as I noted above, the rule of law is enacted through the rule of persons.

Perhaps the most powerful of these intellectual constructions of higher law – and probably the most influential among contemporary legal and political theorists – sought to square the circle by bringing together the rule of law and the rule of citizens within the ideal of a social contract. Emerging in the 17th and 18th centuries as an account of the justification and limits of the powers of the monarch within a state, it takes as its starting point the equal status of human beings as proprietors of themselves and co-possessors of the world. The underlying intuition is that a just political and legal sovereign power would be one to which free and equal individuals could be expected to unanimously consent. Such consent, the theory goes, would be given only to a power that offers fair and equitable mechanisms and rules for securing their common interest to be able to pursue their own good in their own way, freeing them from the uncertainties of mutual harm without itself becoming a source of harm to them. In other words, it tries to unite the political ideal of the equality of virtuous citizens, who rule and are ruled in turn so as to uphold the public interest, with the legal ideal of individuals as rights bearers, who pursue their private interests protected by the rule of law. This argument does not necessarily rest on any actual consent by citizens to generate their obligation to obey a just sovereign. For many theorists in this tradition, it is sufficient that the political and legal system is so organized that we could imagine all citizens *ought to* hypothetically consent to it – or, at least, have no compelling reason not to do so. The idea of a contract is simply a device for thinking about which political and legal arrangements and principles treat people equitably and justly. However, as with theories of God-given or natural law, the terms of the contract are likely to be viewed differently by different theorists, according to the moral and empirical presuppositions they bring to bear in their characterizations of human nature and the causal structure of social relations.

For example, the social contract theories of the 17th-century English philosophers Thomas Hobbes and John Locke portray quite different accounts of human nature and social relations, producing divergent views of what we would consent to. For Hobbes, human beings were apt to pursue their self-interest aggressively and distrust others. Consequently, life outside the state was 'nasty, brutish and short', and they were inclined to consent to any sovereign power capable of offering them security against the risks individuals posed to each other. By contrast, Locke had a much more benign view of the human nature and was inclined to believe that Hobbes underestimated the degree to which state power might be an even greater danger to individual liberty than other individuals. As he put it, Hobbes appeared 'to think, that men are so foolish, that they take care to avoid what mischiefs may be done them by *pole-cats*, or *foxes*; but are content, nay, think it safety, to be devoured by *lions*.' He believed people would only consent to a limited form of government. Such differences as those between Hobbes and Locke indicate that there are liable to be as many views of 'higher law' as there are theorists of it. The disagreements among theorists mirror those between citizens and return us once more to the dilemma that the source of the rule of law will always lie within the rule of persons. That is, that what the rule of law is thought to mean and how that law is interpreted and applied always lies with people.

Modern democracy: uniting political and legal citizenship?

This dilemma confronted the two great revolutions that inaugurated the modern democratic era – the American Revolution of 1776 and the French Revolution of 1789. Both attempted to resolve it by seeing their constitutional settlements as instances of an actual contract between citizens. So, the putative authors of the American Constitution are 'We the People of the United States', while the French Declaration of the Rights of Man and the Citizen declares 'the source of all sovereignty lies essentially in the Nation'. However, these formulas preserve a dualism between the 'public' political citizen, who acts as a collective agent – the 'people' or the 'nation' – and the private, 'legal' citizen, who is the subject of the law and the possessor of 'natural' rights to liberty, property, and the pursuit of happiness. Civic virtue gets assigned to a single constitutional moment and enshrined in the institutions that popular act creates, leaving selfish citizens to pursue their personal interests under the law. Meanwhile, a tension between the two models remains. It is doubtful that even the most well-designed institutions and laws can economize too much on the virtues of citizens, or that citizens feel they are 'theirs' if – the founding moment apart – they cannot actively participate in shaping them.

The political and legal views of citizenship have come to be associated with two traditions of political thought – the republican and the liberal – with many accounts portraying the first as having been slowly displaced by the second. Whereas the republican tradition tends to see liberty as the product of laws that citizens have participated in creating for themselves, liberalism has tended to view law as a necessary evil that should seek to preserve as much of the natural liberty of individuals as is compatible with social life. Nevertheless, such intellectual constructions need to be handled with care. For a start, there have there been numerous varieties of republicanism and liberalism – as we saw, for example, the Greek and Roman views of republican citizenship contained numerous differences, and both these views were subsequently adapted in different ways by later thinkers. Moreover, the two traditions have not only co-existed but became increasingly mixed with the development of democratic nation states during the 19th and 20th centuries. Lying midway between a city state and an empire, the nation state emerged as their most viable alternative – able to combine certain key advantages while avoiding their disadvantages. If the *polis* was too small to survive the military encroachments of empires, the empire was too large to allow for meaningful political participation. The nation state

5. a) Uniting political and legal citizenship: the US Constitution

had sufficient size to sustain both a complex economic infrastructure and an army, while being not so large as to make a credible – if less participatory – form of democracy impossible. As a result, it became subject to pressures to create a form of citizenship that could successfully integrate popular and legal rule by linking political participation and rights with membership of a national democratic political community. It is this development that informs the sociological theories of citizenship, to which we now turn.

5. b) **The French Declaration of the Rights of Man and the Citizen**

The making of modern democratic citizenship

The sociologists T. H. Marshall and Stein Rokkan established what has become the standard narrative of the evolution of modern democratic citizenship. This account draws on their analysis of the history of West European democracies in the 18th, 19th, and 20th centuries. They saw citizenship as the product of the interrelated processes of state-building, the emergence of commercial and industrial society, and the construction of a national consciousness, with all three driven forward in various ways by class struggle and war. Though these three processes tended to be phased, each provided certain of the preconditions for bringing together popular and legal rule within the new context of democratic, welfare, nation states operating within a capitalist market economy.

The first, state-building, phase consisted of administrative, military, and cultural unification at the elite level, accompanied by territorial consolidation and the creation of an elementary, state-wide bureaucratic and legal infrastructure. This phase created a sovereign political body possessing authority over all activities within a given territorial sphere, with those people residing within it becoming its legitimate subjects. The second phase saw the emergence of commercial and industrial economies. This process led to the creation of the infrastructural public goods required by market economies, such as a unified transport system, a standardized system of weights and measures and a single currency, and the establishment of a regular and unitary legal system. Markets also gradually broke down traditional social hierarchies and systems of ascribed status, fostering freedom of contract and equality before the law – particularly with regard to civil and economic rights. The third, nation-making, phase involved the socialization of the masses into a national consciousness suited to a market and industrial economy by means of compulsory education, linguistic standardization, a popular press, and conscript armies. These promoted a common language and guaranteed standards of numeracy and literacy appropriate for a mobile workforce capable of acquiring the generic skills needed for industry. They also helped create affective bonds between both co-nationals themselves and citizens and their state.

The net effect of these three processes was to create a 'people', who were entitled to be treated as equals before the law and possessed equal rights to buy and sell goods, services, and labour; whose interests were overseen by a sovereign political authority; and who shared a national identity that shaped their allegiance to each other and to their state. All three elements became important for democratic citizenship. The first provided the basis for regarding all persons as entitled to the equal protection of the laws – a condition people came to see was unlikely to obtain without an equal right to frame them. The second created a community of interest, most particularly in controlling sufficiently those running the state to ensure that the rulers responded to and promoted the concerns of the ruled rather than oppressing them. The third led citizens to consider themselves as a people, sharing certain common values and various special obligations towards one another. It also fashioned the context for a public sphere in which people could communicate with each other using a common idiom and according to rules and practices that were broadly known and accepted.

In a brilliant essay, T. H. Marshall argued that the citizenship potential offered by the emergence of national markets and nation states had been unleashed by a succession of class struggles. Drawing on the British experience, he contended that there had been three periods in the historical evolution of citizenship. Each period had witnessed the acquisition of a different set of rights and duties by citizens as a given group struggled to attain equal status as a full member of the community. The first period, roughly from the 17th to mid-19th centuries, saw the consolidation of the civil rights needed to engage in a range of social and economic activities, from the freedoms to own property and exchange goods, services, and labour required by a functioning market, to the liberties of thought and conscience necessary to attend a chosen church and to express dissent. The second period, extending from the end of the 18th century to the start of the 20th, coincided with the gaining of political rights to vote and stand for

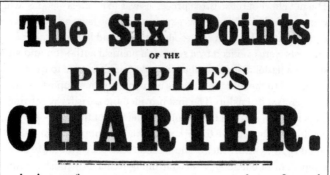

The Six Points

OF THE

PEOPLE'S

CHARTER.

1. A VOTE for every man twenty-one years of age, of sound mind, and not undergoing punishment for crime.

2. THE BALLOT.—To protect the elector in the exercise of his vote.

3. No PROPERTY QUALIFICATION for Members of Parliament —thus enabling the constituencies to return the man of their choice, be he rich or poor.

4. PAYMENT OF MEMBERS, thus enabling an honest trades-man, working man, or other person, to serve a constituency, when taken from his business to attend to the interests of the country.

5. EQUAL CONSTITUENCIES, securing the same amount of representation for the same number of electors, instead of allowing small constituencies to swamp the votes of large ones.

6. ANNUAL PARLIAMENTS, thus presenting the most effectual check to bribery and intimidation, since though a constituency might be bought once in seven years (even with the ballot), no purse could buy a constituency (under a system of universal suffrage) in each ensuing twelvemonth; and since members, when elected for a year only, would not be able to defy and betray their constituents as now.

6. The People's Charter, demanding political rights for working people in 19th-century Britain

election, first by all property owners, then all adult males, and finally women as well. The third period, going from the end of the 19th to the mid-20th century, involved the creation of social rights. Initially, these had consisted simply of 'the right to a modicum of economic welfare and security' but had gradually been extended 'to the right to share to the full in the social heritage and to live the life of a civilised being according to the standards prevailing in society'. So these rights came to include not only social insurance against unemployment or debilitating illness, but also more extensive rights to education, at least up to secondary school, and to health care and pensions.

Marshall's account has come in for considerable criticism. Some have argued that he overlooks the role played by external pressures in promoting rights, others that even in Britain the three sets of rights neither arose in quite the order or periods that he mentions, nor proved quite as complementary as he assumed. Thus, social rights have emerged in most countries before rather than after political rights – indeed, they were often offered by the politically dominant class of the time as a way of damping down demands for political rights. Social rights can also clash with certain civil rights, such as the right to property. However, these corrections to the details of his argument are perfectly compatible with its underlying logic, which remains compelling. Although Marshall has sometimes been read as suggesting that there is an almost inevitable progression from civil to political to ever fuller social rights, this was not his view. He saw the acquisition of rights as a contingent and never-ending struggle. Each phase in the development of rights stems from a subordinate group managing to win concessions from those with power in their fight to be treated with equal concern and respect. In these ways, legal citizenship was altered to encompass new groups through the formal or informal exercise of political citizenship, often by exploiting existing legal rights to gain others. Success in each case came from the ruling classes needing the voluntary cooperation of the ruled to retain their authority. Since different groups can take advantage of different circumstances, the development of citizenship naturally has differed from country to country. For example, the need for mass conscript armies during the First and Second World Wars, and, in consequence, for women's labour to run the domestic economy, aided considerably the acquisition of political and social rights by men and women in many European countries in this period. Yet, in countries such as Spain, Portugal, and Switzerland which remained outside these conflicts, these pressures were absent. As a result, in these countries changes to women's status came by a different and much slower route.

Writing in the 1950s, when the economies of West European countries were in the ascendant and welfare spending expanding, it was natural for Marshall to treat social rights as the culmination of the struggle for an ever more inclusive and egalitarian form of citizenship. Needless to say, subsequent events have tended to challenge that optimistic conclusion. It is not just that many aspects of the post-war welfare settlements Marshall celebrated became eroded during the economic downturn and restructuring of the 1970s, 1980s, and 1990s. Many of the economic and social assumptions on which this settlement rested have also been criticized by those seeking to further expand rather than curtail citizenship. Environmentalists have attacked the emphasis on increasing economic production, feminists its continued overlooking of the subordinate role of women in the labour market, multiculturalists the failure to even mention issues of ethnicity, cosmopolitans its focus on the nation state, and so on. As with the criticisms of Marshall's historical narrative, these observations do not necessarily contradict the main thrust of his argument. They merely indicate how each attempt to realize a form of equal citizenship generates its own unanticipated shortcomings and problems – producing new struggles over the way the political community, rights, and participation are defined.

It is these three sets of struggles and the ways they are altering citizenship that form the subject of the next three chapters. In two respects, current developments may be undermining Marshall's schema. First, legal citizenship has become ever more autonomous from political citizenship as globalization erodes the nation state without creating alternative political communities capable of providing a focus for participation in the promotion of collective goods. For example, international organizations such as the World Bank, the World Trade Organization, and the International Monetary Fund regulate a great deal of international trade, but citizens can control them only very indirectly through their governments. Moreover, such bodies are subject to international law and courts which have very little political accountability at all. Even the EU, which does have direct elections to a special European Parliament, is to a large degree under the control of government executives, on the one hand, and the European Court of Justice, on the other. As Chapter 4 will show, citizenship has been increasingly defined in terms of global human rights to deal with this development. However, the absence of a political dimension suggests that it offers a somewhat second-rate account of what being a citizen involves. Second, and to some extent relatedly, those with power and wealth have become increasingly able to operate without the consent of the comparatively poor and powerless. The more mobile the wealthy become, the harder it is to control their activities and to tax them so they contribute to public goods. As a consequence of these two developments, the capacity for citizenship to be shaped through processes of struggle may have declined.

Chapter 3
Membership and belonging

Membership lies at the heart of citizenship. To be a citizen is to belong to a given political community. However, this link with membership renders citizenship 'exclusive' in ways that have become increasingly controversial. It makes citizens part of a select group, who enjoy privileges denied to non-members. Just as members of an exclusive golf club can use its greens and facilities in ways non-members cannot, so possessing the status of a citizen gives you access to the advantages of membership of a given political community. And just as the rules regulating the membership of golf clubs has often attracted criticism for being inappropriate or discriminatory, so have those conferring the status of citizenship. Indeed, many of the grounds for complaint have been remarkably similar – just as golf clubs have been condemned for limiting membership to well-born, white, rich men, so birth, ethnicity, wealth, and gender have formed the standard – and increasingly contested – criteria for citizenship.

Much like exclusive golf clubs, states have typically justified their exclusions on the grounds that prospective members must be able to contribute in appropriate ways and 'fit in' with existing members and the prevailing ethos. If golf clubs vet prospective members for their ability to pay the fees, prowess at golf, willingness to abide by the club rules and conventions, and their general sociability and likely commitment to club events, so states assess citizens for their potential contribution to the collective goods of the community and their readiness and capacity to abide by its norms and customs. In each case, suspicion arises that the criteria for admission are self-serving and fail to treat all applicants with equal concern and respect. However, an all-important difference exists between golf clubs and political communities. Membership of a political community is for most people both necessary and unavoidable in ways that membership of a golf club is not. The decision to take up golf is a matter of choice, and even dedicated golfers can probably manage to play regularly without belonging to a club or learn to live without it. By contrast, it is virtually impossible not to live in a state. States not only cover most of the earth, but also – as we saw in Chapter 1 – provide the basic structure for a secure and fulfilled life within societies of any complexity. Statelessness almost always results when state failure of one kind or another leads people to flee – be it due to invasion and conquest by another state, civil war, famine, or an oppressive regime. Those in this condition do not live outside any state. Rather, they are forced to become supplicants for whatever aid and support those states willing to receive them, or unable to avoid doing so, condescend to provide.

The necessity and unavoidability of living in a state makes the exclusivity associated with citizenship doubly problematic. First, it seems invidious to exclude those who are subject to a given state's power from full membership, possessing the same rights as other citizens. Second, given that the state you initially find yourself in is an accident of birth, it may seem equally invidious to hinder people moving to become members of a different state that offers them better opportunities, if they are willing to take on the duties as well as enjoy the rights of citizenship. In this chapter, I want to explore these internal and external dimensions of the exclusiveness of citizenship. I shall start by exploring the rationale for the traditional qualifications based on class, property, gender, and ethnicity and the internal challenges that have been posed to each. I shall then examine the exclusion of particular categories of outsiders, setting the scene for a more extensive discussion of global citizenship as going beyond membership of any particular nation or state in Chapter 4. In both cases, much turns on what the duties of citizenship are thought to involve and whether membership requires citizens not simply to play their part but also to belong in some fashion that goes beyond mere duty. As we shall see, the development – charted at the end of the last chapter – of national, democratic, welfare states as the main context for citizenship has allowed the criteria for membership to become progressively more inclusive internally, while remaining externally exclusive.

From subject to citizen: the internal dimension of inclusion and exclusion

I remarked in Chapter 2 how the criteria for citizenship in ancient Greece have cast a long shadow, defining many of the key attributes of the citizen for almost 2,000 years. The Athenian citizen was a householder and property owner, a master of the labour of others, a warrior, of Athenian blood, and male. It seems natural to reject these qualifications out of hand today as unwarranted and discriminatory. Many citizens do not possess any of these qualities – indeed, most citizens lack, or at some stage have lacked, several of them. Yet, there is an underlying rationale to the association of citizenship with these attributes which continues to shape how we think about what it means to be a citizen. So it is worth taking each in turn and pondering how far the reasoning lying behind their historical linkage with citizenship still applies, even if we would no longer relate such arguments to these specific qualities. I shall start with those related to property ownership and then move on to those linked to gender and ethnicity. As we shall see, a more inclusive view of citizenship has largely turned on breaking the connection between these three criteria and the qualities associated with being a citizen.

Property and the properties of citizenship

In ancient Greece, being the patriarch of a household was much more than simply owning a home. The house was the basic component of the economy – indeed, the term 'economy' derives from the Greek words for household (*oikos*) and rules (*nomos*). To be a householder signified being economically self-sufficient, with one's material needs taken care of by a range of domestic servants, not least one's wife as an unpaid household manager. Three features of this condition were deemed important for politics. First, as I mentioned in the last chapter, it meant that citizens could devote themselves to their civic duties, being freed from the need to earn a livelihood. Less plausibly, they were also supposedly above any need to pursue their private interests. Second, they were not only freed from a dependency on things but also from being the dependants of other people. Indeed, they owned others. Of course, they still needed food and so on to survive, and relied on others to provide the necessary goods. But they could direct those others as they chose, sell them if they failed to act as they wished, and so on. Unlike their dependants, they were independent – able to act and think as they believed best rather than as those on whom they depended for their living directed. Finally, it meant they literally had a stake in the political community, with their fate – or at least that of their assets – intimately bound to its fate, to the extent of being willing to fight and possibly die for their country.

These three properties of dedication to the public good, independence, and possession of a stake in the political community remain important for thinking about politics, but over time the qualities associated with them have become detached from the possession of private property. In fact, there has been a general reversal of assumptions: instead of private autonomy being the basis of public autonomy in the political realm, political participation and the regulation of the private sphere have become the guarantees of personal freedom. So, to take the first property of devotion to the public good, we still want to prevent politics being a source of personal gain and becoming either entangled with the private interests of citizens and politicians or having to compete with them for their attention.

However, the way we seek to stop this happening today completely overturns earlier accounts. For example, in line with the thinking that private wealth was a prerequisite for disinterested public service, it was generally thought inappropriate to pay politicians salaries well into the 19th century. Indeed, in Britain it formally remains the case at the local level: it was not until 1974 that a scheme was introduced for paying local councillors allowances for performing various tasks, though subsequent reforms have turned these into salaries in all but name. The aim was to prevent the development of a professional class of politicians. On the one hand, professionalizing politics was thought to undermine the system of citizens taking it in turns to rule and be ruled, creating a political class with a distinct set of sectional interests to those they governed. On the other hand, it was feared payment would turn public service into a means for private enrichment rather than a matter of civic duty – that, as the German sociologist Max Weber put it, politicians would live 'off' rather than 'for' politics. Of course, the flaw in this argument was that politicians could gain far more from making decisions favouring their business interests or those of their friends than any salary. Meanwhile, it effectively debarred those without private wealth from public office. Gradually, starting with those holding government positions, thinking on this score changed to quite the opposite – that a public salary, albeit one often far lower than many politicians could earn in the private sector, was the best means for freeing politicians from their private obligations. Likewise, making politics a profession gave politicians an incentive to develop their political skills and live 'for' politics, achieving success by showing they could lead and act for the public interest.

The innovation that made these changes possible was representative democracy and the system of competing parties.

This development also had implications for the demands placed on citizens. Citizens remain eligible as potential rulers in being able to put themselves forward as candidates for office. But public service is no longer expected of the vast majority of citizens. Instead, the main task for citizens is to select rulers. It is the competition between parties and their alternation in office that allows different groups of citizens, via their elected representatives, to rule and be ruled in turn. The key issue for membership is no longer whether a potential citizen is qualified to rule but rather whether they are qualified to vote and to evaluate the suitability of others for public office. By making political participation far less onerous it comes within the grasp of almost all adults, even though some have argued it thereby becomes so devalued as to be worthless, a point we shall consider in Chapter 5. However, lack of time no longer forms a barrier.

What about self-interest? A common, if not necessarily accurate, criticism of democracy is that citizens vote in self-interested and possibly short-sighted ways. Such considerations have been invoked for curtailing the scope for democratic decision-making and handing certain areas to an allegedly more disinterested and public-spirited elite of 'the great and the good'. Again, we shall return to these issues in Chapter 5. Here it suffices to note that while these concerns still linger, they no longer form a barrier to becoming a citizen – merely to what citizens may be allowed to do. True, there have been arguments that those who draw welfare should be barred from voting because their private interest is closely allied to increasing public spending to which they do not contribute, though in fact this group is among the least likely to vote and has the least influence in society generally. Yet, many have argued that the public interest simply is the aggregate interests of the citizens. Certainly, as we saw in the last chapter, there is a real danger that unless those subject to government are allowed to express their interests politically then they will be overlooked. So rather than seeing the public interest as apart from the private interests of citizens, as was argued in the past, it seems more appropriate now to regard the two as linked, with the one informed by the other, promoting a sense among citizens that their interests are linked to those of the community as a whole.

A similar reversal of assumptions has overturned traditional thinking concerning the second property of the good citizen, independence. Again, the classical view that those who depend on others for their livelihood will lack independence prevailed up to the 19th century, justifying the exclusion of the vast mass of people. However, it had become plain much earlier that this view rested on an anachronistic understanding of the conditions for economic and social 'independence' that none could enjoy. As early as the late 18th century, the Scottish philosopher Adam Smith criticized Jean-Jacques Rousseau's radical defence of the classical position by noting how a central feature of the intensifying of the division of labour allowed by the emerging market society, of which the professionalization of politics was but one example, was that we all became dependent on each other. A 'free man' could no longer be someone who was self-sufficient, the master of an autonomous economic system represented by the household. As civic republican theorists, such as Machiavelli and Rousseau, had always feared, a desire for luxury goods destroyed such independence even for those with considerable wealth. Yet, as Smith pointed out, the universality of mutual dependence also had a certain levelling effect. It created both a normative and a practical foothold for the equalizing of status in both a formal and a substantive sense. In market economies, we all do rather specialist jobs and depend on numerous others to supply our needs. But none of these others are our personal dependants, and it is hard to imagine a situation in a globally organized and complex economy where they could become so. Instead, we must all – even the fabulously rich and powerful – freely contract with others for their goods, labour, and services. In these circumstances of universal mutual dependence, independence is no longer a matter of private wealth but a public achievement of the laws and structures that regulate the conditions under which we contract with others. Since these regulations apply to all, there is a normative presumption that the terms of our mutual dependency should be fair and acknowledge reciprocal rights and duties of equal respect and concern.

In Chapter 2, I noted that the idea of political society as itself the product of a contract offers a powerful theoretical tool for modelling such a fair social and political system. Freedom of contract also had important practical consequences, eventually allowing workers to organize and use their bargaining power to equalize first the terms and conditions of their employment and then their legal standing in other areas too, including politics. The key became to ensure all citizens could make decisions for themselves rather than having to defer to another's opinion because they depended on them entirely for their livelihood and information. At least a part of the rationale behind rights to education and welfare, for example, is that they secure people's independence as citizens by removing such dependence. The former enables citizens to access and assess information for themselves, the latter means they are never entirely at the mercy of another for the necessities of life. Moreover, the justification for publicly supporting these measures stems from duties of reciprocity between citizens that again follow from their condition of mutual dependence.

Of course, even with this public support, there may be some who remain in a natural state of dependency. Children are excluded from full citizenship on the grounds that they have yet to develop the capacity of independent reasoning or living on their own, and are necessarily dependent on the views and support of their parents. The mentally ill or disabled tend to be excluded on similar grounds. Even these categories of exclusion have prompted controversy. However, on the whole, criticism has been about grey areas, such as whether children become capable of intellectual and economic independence – and hence should qualify for the vote – at 21, 18, or, as has been recently proposed in the UK, 16, rather than as a result of rejecting the notion of independence outright.

Just as private property no longer seems a guarantee of devotion to the public good or independence, so – for related reasons – it can also be questioned how well it serves the third property of citizenship and provides evidence of a stake in the political community. Again, this argument persisted well into the 19th century. For example, it was at the heart of one of the earliest discussions of the principle of votes for all – the Putney Debates of 1647 during the English Civil War.

7. The Putney Debates, October to November 1647

Certain factions in the army that had supported Parliament against the King believed that even common soldiers had earned a right to political liberty. In a famous defence of political equality, Colonel Rainsborough, the most articulate of the 'Leveller' faction, as it came to be known, argued 'that the poorest he that is in England hath a life to live, as the greatest he; and therefore ... the poorest man in England is not bound in a strict sense to that government that he hath not had a voice to put himself under'. The response of the 'grandees' gathered around Cromwell reflected the conventional wisdom of the time. Speaking on their behalf, Henry Ireton retorted that 'no person hath a right to an interest or share in the disposing of the affairs of the kingdom, and in determining or choosing those that shall determine what laws we shall be ruled by here – ... that hath not a permanent fixed interest in this kingdom'. And, he implied, the most tangible sign of such 'a permanent fixed interest' was ownership of part of its territory – in other words, landed property. Yet, the link between property ownership and a concern with the long-term interests of the wider community has always been a contingent and partial one, and in today's globalized economy where key assets are owned by foreign investors has become even more dubious. It all depends how far the owners will benefit from any positive effects their use of those assets may have for their fellow citizens or share with them any ill effects of their activities. Unfortunately, this is often not the case and they can gain more from exploiting their property in ways that damage the 'permanent fixed interests' of the wider community. The classic example is pollution. Unless environmentally friendly policies benefit the owners of a company – either by enhancing their profits or because they themselves are adversely affected by unfriendly policies – then they will have no incentive to pursue them, and indeed often do not for this very reason.

However, if property is a poor guide to whether a citizen's interests are tied to those of the political community, some sign of long-term commitment does seem appropriate. After all, citizens not only derive benefits from the state but also can influence its future shape through the decisions they make. Many states have therefore made a significant period of continuous residence a criterion for full citizenship – not just for immigrants wishing to naturalize, but also for those who are citizens by birth, with the latter losing certain rights if they choose to reside elsewhere. Certainly, residence offers a more tangible sign than property ownership that one is committed to pursuing policies that will not adversely affect fellow citizens because they will impact equally on you.

Nevertheless, a problem remains – to be explored below – that those affected by many state policies may reside outside its borders. Environmental measures once again offer a telling example. Thus, a policy forcing factories to construct tall chimneys, say, may be good news for local residents, but effectively exports the noxious emissions to those living across the border. As a result, some have argued that we should be treated as citizens of whatever political organization affects us. However, whereas sharing a reasonably delimited territorial space means we will be affected to a fairly substantial degree by the whole range of government measures, only a few selective policies will have a significant impact on those outside the borders. True, even within states there is some differentiation between issues that are best decided at a local level, because they can be most effectively organized by and need only affect a fairly small region, such as dustbin collection, and issues that are decided nationally, such as defence.

Moreover, in Britain and other countries, many people qualify as local citizens on the basis of residence, and vote in local elections, even if they do not meet the more demanding criteria for national citizenship. Yet, consideration is given to the knock-on effects of local policies for national ones and *vice versa* by virtue of the national political community encompassing the local, with full citizens having voting rights in both. By contrast, giving Danish citizens, say, a vote on certain British environmental policies because measures such as tall chimneys result in acid rain that pollutes their lakes, would be inequitable if they were able to distort the political agenda so that spending on environmental protection to benefit Danes undermined national health or educational policies benefiting British citizens as a whole. Such problems might be got round if one could regard issues that affect a global political community as somehow encompassing national policies, but as the experience of the EU suggests, matters are not so neat.

Meanwhile, mere residence or being affected may not in themselves offer a sufficient stake in a political community to motivate people to try and ensure that its policies are efficient and effective if they do not have to pay for them. When the American colonists declared independence, they did so in large part on the basis of the slogan that there should be 'no taxation without representation'. But, as I noted above, it was long thought that the reverse should equally hold true – that those who did not pay taxes ought not to be represented. Otherwise, they would have no motive to encourage governments to pursue cost-effective policies. Similar reasoning has led some to argue that one should disenfranchise the elderly, who may have incentives not to save for the future – say, by greatly raising spending on their pensions, which are paid for by the subsequent generation. Of course, most pensioners have children and hence an interest in their future. Likewise, those on welfare gain in other ways from efficient government policies and have an interest in the economy remaining strong enough to be able to pay their benefits. Moreover, many argue that they have a duty to at least be potential contributors to state revenues by being available for work, willing to go on training courses, and so on. Such arguments lie behind workfare or 'mutual obligation' schemes in the United States, Canada, and Australia. This view that to qualify for citizenship you should be not just affected by policies but also contribute to sustaining them follows from the notion of reciprocity that lies at the heart of national welfare states – that citizens cooperate to sustain the public goods that are provided by a political association. Criminals are excluded from citizenship precisely on the grounds that they have broken this social contract, though this practice has become increasingly controversial – especially in the United States, where convicted felons are sometimes disenfranchised permanently and not just for the period of their imprisonment.

For a long time the most tangible sign of a willingness to align one's interests with the state and do one's bit to uphold it was military service. Moreover, republican theorists worried that if rulers could use mercenaries or create a professional army, then they would be able to dominate the ruled. A citizen's army was a necessary complement to democracy to keep rulers in check. Note, this argument does not imply an individual 'right' to bear arms so much as a citizen's duty to participate in the defence of the country – a point implicit in the Second Amendment to the US Constitution's association of this right with the need for a 'well-regulated militia', though lost in subsequent debates. All these ideas lay behind the Levellers' demands reported above. So, it may seem odd to include this topic under the heading of property. Yet, in ancient and medieval times, the only warriors who counted were those who could arm themselves or raise and fund an army from among their dependants. Even as armies became professionalized during the 17th and 18th centuries, few ordinary soldiers enlisted willingly but had to be coerced into service and had to purchase their weapons from their pay. Once again, a major change came about in the late 19th and early 20th centuries with the need for mass armies. The introduction of universal male adult suffrage and the conscription of all fit adult males more or less went hand in hand. Requiring the ultimate sacrifice without granting some say over when it might be demanded and what one was fighting for became untenable, particularly in light of the mass slaughter of the First World War. This event reaffirmed the importance of the old republican view of citizenship and military service, albeit in a much more inclusive form that once again de-privatized the right to bear arms by disassociating it from having property in one's weapons. Meanwhile, it has become ever more redundant as wars have returned to being fought by professional armies and even to rely on private security firms, though this development potentially revives the classic republican worries about the separation of citizenship and the right and duty to fight.

Like all the other shifts noted above, this change initially affected men alone. Moreover, it was accompanied by, and largely assumed, a more thoroughgoing cultural identification with the state stemming from nationality – only patriots, it was thought, would be prepared to die for their country. Accordingly, the rest of this section explores how far the criteria for citizenship explored so far involve a gender and cultural bias.

Gender and the feminist critique

Many of the traditional attributes of citizenship have been associated with male roles, such as soldiering, from which women were excluded. This fact has produced a two-pronged feminist critique of the way citizenship has come to be defined and practised. First, feminists have argued that the public practice of citizenship has often rested on the private domination of women. Second, they have argued that citizenship has been conceived in terms of masculine qualities.

The first criticism is undeniable. Both in the past and to some extent today, men have turned women into personal dependants, whom they can treat as unpaid domestic servants and direct as they will. Economic dependency resulting from the man being the main 'bread-winner' and, up to the 19th century, coming into possession of his wife's assets on marriage, was often reinforced by coercion, including the legally sanctioned use of physical force – marital rape, for example, was not recognized in law or criminalized until well into the 20th century in many jurisdictions. Control of women's domestic labour allowed 'male' jobs, including politics, to be so structured that the maintenance of a home and raising a family became factored out as not being a post-holder's responsibility. Despite major legislative changes over the past 100 years – from women obtaining equal voting rights to men in almost all established democracies by the mid-20th century, to anti-discrimination and equal pay legislation passed during the second half of that century – caring roles remain largely unpaid and under-supported, and still fall mainly to women. As a result, women predominate in low-paid, part-time jobs, and are under-represented and less well rewarded in most senior management positions. A recent survey in the UK revealed that women who work part-time earn, on average, 38% less per hour than men working full-time. Even women working full-time earn 17% less per hour relative to full-time men. Politics is no exception – indeed, it performs rather worse than many professions. Fewer than 20% of British Members of Parliament are women, for example, and – at the time of writing – only 5 out of the 22 paid members of the Cabinet, the 23rd unpaid member being the female Minister for Housing. With the exception of the Scandinavian countries, where women comprise around 40% of the legislature, most democracies fare little better – indeed many, such as the United States, where only 16% of national politicians are women, do considerably worse.

How can this situation be altered, and what are its implications for how we think about politics? In particular, does de-gendering citizenship involve a distinctively feminist approach to politics? The claim that we require a new approach typically centres on the feminist slogan 'the personal is the political'. At one level, this points to the need for a change of social attitudes that involves action outside the formal channels of politics – for example, through women challenging male assumptions that child care or cleaning are 'women's' work, that is either beneath them or for which they are somehow unsuited. At another level, it indicates how we cannot see politics as resting on a pre-political private sphere. On the contrary, politics and its preconditions are themselves politically and publicly constructed. Marriage, after all, is a legal relationship and the law can enter the bedroom to decree rape unlawful. Likewise, ensuring employers have an obligation to grant maternity and paternity leave and providing state funding for child care are public measures that will to some degree restructure personal relationships. Both of these developments will clearly help women participate as citizens and politicians, hopefully altering prejudices to choosing women candidates and making the political workplace more compatible with men and women sharing domestic and family responsibilities. Equally clearly, as the figures reported above indicate all too starkly, change will only come with sustained and concerted public effort, and even then will be painfully slow.

Significant though both these ways of conceiving the 'personal as political' are for women, they reflect the general historical trajectory the understanding of citizenship has taken rather than being distinctively 'feminist'. As I noted in Chapter 1, it is now common to employ an enlarged view of citizenship that encompasses our broader social and moral obligations to others. As I also remarked, important though social morality is for politics, there is nonetheless a distinctive role to be played by collective decision-making within the formal political process of the state. The key change in this regard has been the recognition that giving women the personal freedom in the private sphere necessary for them to be able to participate on an equal basis to others is in fact a public matter – it results from putting in place a fair system of public rules and collective policies that encourage the sharing of domestic tasks and does not discriminate against individuals taking on caring roles for children or the elderly and so on. Yet, we have seen how this reversal of assumptions, whereby private autonomy does not provide the basis for participation in the public sphere but is rather the product of such participation, parallels precisely the route taken by the property-less. For they too had to overcome the private barriers to their public

8. Marching for women's suffrage, New York City, 1913 (top), and a May Day workers' rights demonstration, New York, 2000 (bottom)

involvement by organizing for better working conditions, education, welfare, and so on – challenging in their turn the view that such issues were purely non-political.

The second feminist argument, that citizenship needs to be understood in feminine rather than masculine terms, is more controversial. Historically, women have been viewed as unsuited to citizenship on the grounds that they are too emotional – ruled by their passions rather than reason, and liable to be partial to those for whom they feel particular attachments rather than acting impartially. The claim of some, though far from all, feminists is that reason, impartiality, and universalism are indeed masculine ways of thinking, and that women take a more 'caring' approach centred on affection and feeling for particular others. Yet, because men and women have never been on a completely equal footing with each other, it is impossible to know which attitudes result from any possible differences in their nature and what is simply the product of cultural and social norms. As it is, there are women and men on both sides of this debate about the character of moral and political reasoning. Indeed, discussion of the appropriate role and balance between universal accounts of rights and justice, on the one hand, and more particular, affective ties of duty, on the other, largely shapes the other major issue surrounding membership – namely, how far citizenship should be limited to co-nationals who share certain ethnic or cultural characteristics.

Nationality, ethnicity, and multiculturalism

As we have seen, the development of a more inclusive account of citizenship rested on the emergence of publicly supported democratic welfare systems. Historically, these systems arose in the context of state- and nation-building. A key issue today concerns how far this connection between democracy and welfare, on the one hand, and the nation state, on the other, was a matter of historical contingency that can now be overcome.

The argument that nation-building is an inherent aspect of a democratic welfare system rests on the alleged contribution of national sentiment in creating solidarity and trust, while facilitating more generally the capacity of citizens to frame and sustain collective policies. Solidarity and trust are vital to any cooperative endeavour and are mutually reinforcing. Democracy assumes a people, or *demos*, who feel sufficient solidarity with each other to accept collective decisions and enough mutual trust to cooperate. Without solidarity, individuals would be tempted to obey only those collective decisions that benefited them and even then might be inclined to free-ride. Majorities may be unwilling to accommodate minorities, minorities to accept majority decisions. Without trust, the fear will be that nobody will play their part – that, for example, if an incumbent government concedes defeat in an election their successors will prevent their ever winning again, thereby justifying their rigging or halting the electoral process themselves to stay in power. Welfare similarly depends on the 'haves' showing solidarity towards the 'have-nots' and trust in the former doing their best to improve the conditions of the latter and, if successful, to shoulder a part of the burden in their turn. Finally, making collective decisions assumes common institutions, customs, and discourses that all involved agree are legitimate and can employ.

A common nationality is said to foster solidaristic and trusting feelings by creating a common identity that draws on a shared culture, history, and language. These commonalities supposedly create a bond between people that reaches beyond their many differences of opinion and interests and enables them to cooperate with each other. This claim is partly sociological, partly normative, and partly functional. First, people find it easier to engage with and trust those whom they regard as similar in certain pertinent ways. Second, cooperative activities, such as democracy and welfare, involve more than the humanitarian obligations we owe to people in general, important though these are. They entail a high degree of reciprocity between people and the sort of special obligations to particular others that exist among family members and good neighbours. Not only are such obligations difficult to create and sustain among all human beings, but also people of differing cultures will want to shape them in different ways. Last, but far from least, a shared language and political traditions greatly facilitate communication and decision-making, making it easier for all to participate on equal terms and reducing the scope for misunderstanding or incompatibility clashes.

On this account, therefore, nationality defines citizenship. It provides the social glue and medium that enables citizens to interact on equal terms in the life of the political community. Yet, while state-building and nation-building went hand in hand in the past, there are obvious problems in drawing too tight a connection between the two. It is estimated that there are between 5,000 and 9,000 ethnic-cultural groups in the world, and only around 200 states, over 90% of which contain more than one ethnic group. To overcome this diversity, nation-building in the past involved some or all of the following: genocide, forced mass-population transfers, coerced assimilation, and domination and control by the ruling group. With most states being formed through war and conquest, indigenous peoples and minority national, religious, ethnic, and linguistic groups have all suffered from these sorts of oppression, as have later immigrant minorities. No respectable advocate of nationalism today believes that such methods are in any way acceptable. Instead, they argue that a common nationality can not only accommodate diversity but makes it possible.

How can that be? First, they argue that if people are to interact effectively then some common structures are going to be necessary. So there will need to be broad acceptance that the existing legal and political institutions are, if not perfect, nevertheless the appropriate mechanism through which any change must take place – including changes to those institutions themselves. Second, there must also be the desire to engage with co-citizens on equal terms and to frame common laws and policies

9. A citizenship ceremony in Australia, 2005

in ways that can be justified as reasonable to all. Such requirements are consistent with citizens giving their allegiance to the state, having some knowledge of its political history and institutions, being reasonably fluent in its main language or languages, and having an appreciation of the cultural conventions and sensibilities of its members. Indeed, Western democracies have increasingly codified these elements of a common national citizenship, enshrining them both in tests and ceremonies for the acquisition of citizenship and in the teaching of citizenship in schools.

Typically, these policies have arisen as responses to fears of growing multicultural unrest and violence and concerns over rising rates of immigration. As a result, they have attracted criticism in certain quarters as perpetuating rather than diminishing discrimination towards minority groups, with some arguing such policies should be replaced by considerations based on human rights norms and international law. I shall consider these arguments more fully in the next chapter. However, the short response from the nationalist would be that rights norms will always need to be realized within a given cultural context, which fleshes them out in specific ways. Moreover, such acculturation will never be neutral in its effects. Choices will have to be made about public holidays, the official language(s), and so on that will inevitably impact on some minorities more than others.

However, the discriminatory effects of such decisions can be mitigated in all sorts of ways. There can be exemptions from laws that penalize certain cultural practices, such as the British exemption of Sikhs from the wearing of motorcycle helmets. There can be assistance for minorities to overcome certain disadvantages, from state support for cultural activities, including the funding of religious schools as in the UK, to affirmative action, and the symbolic recognition of their acceptance – for example, through multi-faith policies for religious education and public ceremonies. There can be the devolution of certain self-government rights to national minorities, as is the case with the Scots, Welsh, and Northern Irish in the UK, and indigenous groups, such as the Inuit in Canada, and/or special representation (also for immigrant communities) in public bodies, as is the case for the Maori in New Zealand. There can be multilingual policies and even the allowance of parallel legal systems, as occurs with the Welsh and Scots respectively. Most states adopt some of these policies, and traditional countries of immigration, such as Australia, Canada, and the United States, have tended to adopt almost all of them, as has the UK.

The purpose of these policies is to render the notion of a common national citizenship more inclusive, creating a sense of belonging among the very diverse groups that make up modern societies. To return to the image of a social contract, they reflect the attempt for citizens to negotiate mutually acceptable norms of political cooperation that better reflect their civic equality. Yet, some commentators have criticized these measures as undermining the whole citizenship project – detracting from equal status and fragmenting civic identities, with a consequent loss of solidarity and trust and a reduction in participation. France, which has a strong tradition of republican civic identity, has tended to take this line, but it has also been endorsed by many liberals as well. However, the empirical evidence tends to suggest the reverse, with policies promoting a common national citizenship proving more acceptable where they are accompanied with an equally clear commitment to multiculturalism and diversity. The partial exception is with territorially concentrated minorities, where devolved institutions can strengthen rather than weaken demands for greater independence and even succession, as has proved the case in Quebec in Canada and Scotland in the UK, although if successful the new countries would have to confront many of the self-same issues of diversity.

Moreover, in any polity there are limits to how much accommodation is possible, notably when minority practices are deemed to infringe human rights. For example, Western democracies have outlawed such practices as so-called female circumcision. However, numerous hard cases exist, particularly with regard to the education of children and attitudes towards women, who have a subordinate role in many cultures. In these cases, a potential tension exists between the maintenance of certain traditional practices and protecting the opportunity for children, and particularly women, to choose whether they abide by traditional norms or adapt or even drop them altogether, exploring instead the wider possibilities open to them in the broader community. These tensions have been resolved in different ways in different countries, but the sign of a commitment to common citizenship derives from all affected parties seeking solutions that are capable of being justified in mutually acceptable terms. In these ways, a national citizenship ceases to be something imposed by a dominant group on others but a shared civic project, involving a degree of compromise and adaptation on all sides.

From alien to citizen: the external dimension of exclusion

So far I have defined being a citizen in terms of certain properties – notably, a linking of one's private interests and the public interest, including a commitment to the country and a willingness to contribute to its economic, social, and political public goods by working, paying taxes, and voting, and a capacity to evaluate political performance and exercise independent judgements. I have also noted that extending such properties to all relies on seeing them as public rather than private responsibilities, while their joint exercise is facilitated by a sense of common nationality. Finally, I have claimed seeing citizenship in these terms need not discriminate against women or minority cultures and nationalities. Instead, they have been able progressively to reshape national political cultures to reflect their claims to civic equality. Perhaps the crucial test of their success, though, is how far the resulting membership criteria offer defensible grounds for admission for would-be immigrants.

This issue has become increasingly salient as migratory pressures have grown. Reliable figures are hard to come by, but it is estimated there were around 150 million migrants in 2000 – double the number in 1965. Of course, there have been periods of massive migration in the past. But the global scope, variety, and sustained volume of contemporary migratory trends are unprecedented. Some of this pressure has come from asylum seekers, driven out of their countries by war or oppression. Though a grey line often divides the two, I want to separate this group – whom countries have a humanitarian, and in the case of signatories of the Geneva Convention on the Status of Refugees (1951) and its 1967 Protocol, a legal duty to assist – from immigrants seeking a different or better life. The key issue is whether it is legitimate for governments to limit rising demands from this second group.

All wealthy, democratic countries do limit immigration, usually through having residence requirements to show commitment, normally of around three to four years, a language test, and a test on national history, customs, and institutions, and have favoured those with desirable economic skills, such as doctors. These conditions codify the properties outlined above that have traditionally been thought necessary for someone to be a full member of the political community. How far they are perceived as discriminatory depends on the context and manner in which they are imposed. If the country is seen as generally welcoming to immigrants from all countries, not favouring ethnically and culturally similar groups, and there is public support for meeting the language and other test requirements, the required language skills are basic and the questions on politics and culture are reasonably straightforward and could be answered by most existing citizens, not being designed in such a way as to force all immigrants to renounce pre-existing identities and affiliations, then these conditions can enjoy broad support, or at least be uncontroversial, even among immigrant communities. For example, in Canada, where citizenship and immigration policy has become increasingly open since the 1960s, these policies have been largely, if not universally, accepted as legitimate and legitimating – making it easier rather than harder for immigrants to feel full members of their new country. There, the external citizenship criteria for immigrants are but the counterpart to a broader and more multicultural internal citizenship policy. By contrast, when set against a background of suspicion towards immigrants tinged with racism, as tends to be the case with former colonial powers, such as Britain, these policies can be met with suspicion and regarded as exclusionary – a fear reinforced in recent times by seemingly panicked responses by some governments to the emerging link between immigrant communities and terrorism. By and large, attempts to allay the potential fears of native-born citizens have tended to backfire, appearing to give such worries credence while alienating the immigrant communities and exacerbating social tensions.

Such failures have tended to bring the whole linkage between citizenship and membership of a nation state into disrepute. So long as this link exists, however, it will be justified to limit admission to citizenship by criteria that reflect the attributes necessary for participation in a national political community. Yet, some commentators have argued this connection is simply untenable, both practically and morally, in our increasingly globalized societies. Instead, they seek to define citizenship in terms of universal human rights. It is to the degree to which such a definition is normatively and practically possible that I now turn.

Chapter 4
Rights and the 'right to have rights'

Citizenship is often identified with rights. In a trivial sense, this identification always exists because whatever citizenship policies a given country puts in place will bestow the equivalent rights on citizens. Such rights are generally called 'positive' or 'institutional' rights. For example, British citizenship is defined by the various rights associated with the numerous policies ordaining who is a citizen and what they are entitled to: from the Nationality, Immigration and Asylum Act 2002, governing processes of naturalization, to the Representation of the People Act 2000, covering voting arrangements, and the various Social Security Acts, dealing with unemployment, sickness, maternity, pensions, and other benefits. These and similar pieces of legislation all spell out the rights that follow from the status of being a British citizen – from voting to welfare. However, the details of these rights differ from country to country and possibly even within a country. The rights of English citizens are not identical in every respect to those of Scottish citizens, say, and differ even more from those of American or French citizens. Moreover, they need not be either just or equitable – even Nazi laws conferred certain rights on German citizens, although they also condemned many to being less than citizens.

Consequently, when people invoke rights as the basis of citizenship, they generally intend something rather different. They mean that citizens *ought* to have the positive or institutional rights that follow from what they believe to be people's moral or human rights. Indeed, almost all countries have enshrined at least some of these sorts of rights in constitutional documents that are deemed superior to ordinary legislation, thereby allowing citizens to criticize existing positive rights for failing to live up to their human or moral rights as individuals, at least in so far as these are understood and protected by the relevant constitutional court. On these accounts, rights provide the basis for citizenship, with the development of citizenship policies being driven by the steady, if often halting, realization of these rights in ever fuller ways. More importantly, rights are offered as an alternative and more just way of thinking about citizenship to membership of a national political community. The United States is often taken as the model of such a rights-based national identity. A society of mass immigration, adherence to the Constitution has often been portrayed as defining what it means to be an American citizen. Yet, appealing to the Constitution has also proved a mechanism for altering the terms of citizenship in important ways, as in the civil rights movement of the 1960s which saw the progressive expansion of the terms of American citizenship to include black Americans on a more equitable basis.

Popular and apparently attractive though such accounts are, however, they suffer from two related difficulties, both of which point to a potential tension between citizenship and rights. First, if rights are universal, applying to all human beings, then a possible conflict exists between being a citizen of a particular political community and upholding rights. Justice arguably demands we treat all human beings with equal concern and respect, a position that – if true – could be at variance with treating one's fellow citizens with greater regard to everyone else. Cosmopolitan or global citizenship possibly offers a solution, yet holds practical and normative problems of its own – as we shall see. Second, although there is a growing consensus around the idea of human rights, a consensus linked to a commitment to freedom and equality that lies at the heart of the citizenship ideal, a great deal of scope exists for disagreement about which rights best realize these values and the policy implications that flow from them. As I noted in Chapter 1, democratic citizenship has offered a way of overcoming such disagreements, with citizenship paradoxically offering its own foundation – the right to have rights. Yet, democracy could clash with rights if majorities seek to promote their own interests at the expense of minorities, thereby making it a right to suppress rather than promote rights. The rest of this chapter explores both these issues in turn.

Human rights and cosmopolitan citizenship

Human rights concern how we ought to treat our fellow human beings. Various sources have been given for these rights – from God-given natural law to human nature, history or reason, with these sources being associated with a variety of moral values and principles. Here is not the place to evaluate these different theories, many of which no longer enjoy wide currency. It suffices to note how, despite their many differences, those theories taken seriously today attempt to articulate the basic intuition that all human beings are entitled to be treated with a degree of concern and respect. As a result, there are certain things that nobody should do to another human being, and we should seek to secure for all the basic conditions needed to live a decent life. On the one hand, therefore, rights seek to constrain what we may do to other people. Such rights include the standard civil rights against such acts as being assaulted or tortured, or being detained or punished without a due process. On the other hand, rights indicate the need for support rather than just forbearance. Socio-economic rights to minimum standards of health, education, and subsistence are often characterized in this way.

It is sometimes argued that the first type of right is capable of being universalized in ways that the second type is not. Each one of us can respect the rights not to be raped, murdered, and so on of everyone in the world by simply refraining from such actions. But it would soon exhaust even the richest person's resources to attempt to provide succour for all those in need, while to give to some but not to others seems arbitrary. Those who take this line generally recognize a humanitarian duty to aid those in distress when it lies in one's power to do so at little or no risk to oneself. Most people accept that a wealthy country that failed to provide relief to victims of a natural disaster, say, would be as culpable as a good swimmer who failed to go to the aid of a drowning child in a swimming pool. However, they argue any fuller application of this type of right arises only when someone has a special responsibility to help particular others – such as those I have a duty to protect, like my children; those who I may have intentionally or unintentionally harmed in some way; or those with whom I have explicitly engaged to provide such rights, such as my fellow citizens. From this perspective, no tension need exist between recognizing human rights while acknowledging a fuller set of citizenship rights to fellow members of your political community. So long as your country does not coerce the citizens of other countries and has some kind of aid budget for global emergencies, then it has fulfilled its responsibilities.

However, many people contend matters are not quite so clear cut. For a start, the poverty and poor health experienced in much of the undeveloped or developing world does not arise simply from misfortune, such as floods, droughts, or earthquakes. It also results from the systematic commercial exploitation of poor by affluent countries and their direct or indirect support of coercive regimes. The globalization of production and exchange means that most citizens of the developed world cannot avoid being complicit to some degree in this exploitation or benefiting from it. So a responsibility exists to help the world's poor and oppressed that goes beyond a duty of humanitarian aid. It is also the case that even upholding rights not to be physically coerced requires more than merely refraining from such actions. Regrettably, there are always some individuals prepared to take advantage of others. Just as social and economic rights require hospitals, schools, a social security system, and so on, so civil rights require a legal system, police force, and prisons, among other things – all of which can be just as costly. And because national systems increasingly interact with each other, while much economic and social activity – including crime – is transnational, we need international arrangements and bodies to uphold both sets of rights.

A natural response to this circumstance has been to propose a form of cosmopolitanism. A doctrine going back to the ancient world and associated particularly with the Roman stoics, a cosmopolitan is literally a 'citizen of the world' or *kosmopolitai*. The Greek derivation of this term suggests that world citizenship implies a world polity or *kosmos* [world] *polis*. Yet, such an arrangement raises such clear problems that very few contemporary advocates of cosmopolitanism propose it – at least explicitly. They have tended to associate the cosmopolitan ideal with the Roman imperial notion of 'legal citizenship' rather than the Greek conception of 'political citizenship'. However, the disadvantages confronting a world 'legal citizenship' can be just as formidable. We'll explore each in turn.

Although various schemes have been put forward for different kinds of cosmopolitan polity, creating a meaningful system of global democracy that could provide the setting for a political form of world citizenship faces considerable obstacles. Size matters, and the larger the scale on which democracy works, the less influence citizens will have and the more disempowered they are likely to feel. Many citizens of the larger democracies express such feelings already, but in any type of world democracy representatives would need to be responsible for millions rather than thousands of voters. As we shall see in Chapter 5, this problem can be overcome to some extent where there are sufficient commonalities among the electorate for groups of voters to be able to combine their preferences into a few reasonably coherent ideological programmes, none of which is completely incompatible with the others. These conditions allow citizens to feel adequately represented by one of the available parties, and not entirely excluded even if their preferred party is in opposition. However, where there are deep divisions – especially of an ethnic or cultural nature – then it is much more likely that electoral minorities will feel alienated and may even be oppressed. As a result, they will seek as much autonomy as possible from central government control.

Diversity of this divisive kind is already proving a growing problem within most existing states – witness the growing separatist tendency of given cultural groups in such established democracies as Canada and Belgium, where a high percentage of citizens in the French- and Flemish-speaking regions respectively have supported parties seeking to secede from their country – and is likely to be even more problematic within the world as a whole. Despite traditional liberal views that culture and religion should be – and would become – purely personal issues, of no relevance for politics, they have remained stubbornly central to the efficient working of most political systems. Some analysts contend that globalization will overcome this difficulty by homogenizing cultures to a degree, giving everyone a taste for designer jeans, cappuccinos, cola, and McDonald's. But though these processes have diffused good- as well as poor-quality products, bringing cosmopolitan tastes to far more people than ever before, few would regard the replacement of cultural variety with mass consumerism as an entirely enticing – or likely – prospect. In fact, part of the attractiveness of a system of separate states lies precisely in allowing different cultures to thrive. Meanwhile, the existence of alternative regimes also puts pressure on despotic states in particular to improve their ways – not least because they offer a possible place of escape for opponents and others. As the 18th-century German philosopher Immanuel Kant, who inspires most contemporary cosmopolitan thought, acknowledged, because a world state gets rid of such alternatives, it risks being 'a universal despotism'.

As a result, like Kant, most cosmopolitans favour a system of states which have bound themselves by a series of international agreements to abide by certain universal principles of justice as embodied in international law – particularly rights charters such as the United Nation's Universal Declaration of Human Rights (1948) and the European Convention on Human Rights (1950). In Kant's scheme, individual states remain the primary sources of political authority. However, a number of neo-Kantian cosmopolitans have argued that state sovereignty has been undermined nonetheless by the global moral obligations that stem from human rights. State boundaries and our attachments to them are morally arbitrary and no preference ought to be given to co-nationals in the distribution of resources needed to uphold either civil or social rights. Though it may be convenient to partition political authority into local units, it is subject to an international legal authority and must be employed to further cosmopolitan ends.

This account makes cosmopolitanism rather like a more just version of the Roman imperial view of legal citizenship we encountered in Chapter 2. However, it runs into a number of parallel problems to those we noted with that argument – not least in its similar downgrading of political citizenship. First, we tend to understand rights through the prism of the different cultural, moral, ideological, and other beliefs that we hold about what is important in life and how societies work. There may be considerable, if not complete, agreement in the abstract about certain basic rights, but there is much less about what actually follows from them in practice. Different views of moral responsibility or social causality, for example, will produce differing and even conflicting views of when a right has been infringed or not, and by whom. For instance, such differences will inform arguments about the positive or negative effects of free markets with regard to certain social problems – influencing judgements as to how far the poor are 'freely' contracting for their low wages, say, or entrepreneurs are responsible for either their own profits or the welfare of their suppliers, workers, or customers. Yet, all the parties to this dispute may agree on the importance of civil rights to non-interference. Likewise, those who are religious will regard the practices required by religious belief as generating rights in ways that those who do not share such beliefs will not. However, both the religious and the non-religious may believe in the importance of rights to freedom of self-expression and of thought – they simply disagree as to whether they apply in a given case or not. Given the size and diversity of the globe compared to any state, these sorts of empirical and normative disagreements are likely to be far greater for any cosmopolitan arrangement than they are for national ones.

Second, these disagreements mean that under a purely legal scheme of cosmopolitan citizenship, international courts will have to make highly controversial normative and empirical judgements when deciding if a given individual's rights have been infringed or not. Of course, domestic courts also often find themselves having to make similarly controversial decisions. However, they do so in the light of a large body of domestic case law that has been shaped by the evolving national political culture – including the host of formal and informal pressures that politicians, the media, and the general public bring to bear on the judiciary over time. Indeed, studies show that even apparently highly controversial court decisions align well with long-term trends of sustained, majority, national public opinion. For the reasons we explored above regarding the difficulty of establishing a world government, it is much harder to gauge world public opinion or for it to exert any influence. Moreover, greater diversity heightens the danger of majority tyranny over various minority views. International human rights charters are often derided – whether fairly or not – as the wish-lists of unrepresentative pressure groups. To overcome such criticism and command the resources they need to be effective, rights need to be able to win widespread political support. After all, if legal decisions are to be complied with, then

10. A session of the International Court of Justice

people must be able to identify with them. Democracy offers the standard mechanism for amicably settling differences and arriving at workable compromises to produce legislation citizens can view as in some sense theirs. Unfortunately, as we have seen, the preconditions for such a system simply are not available at the global level.

We seem faced with a conundrum. Justice appears to demand linking citizenship to rights within some form of cosmopolitan scheme. Yet, a legal form of rights-based citizenship risks being too controversial to command the legitimacy and support needed for it to work, while a form of political citizenship that might provide it with the necessary authority seems unworkable on a world scale. Is there a way, therefore, of linking rights, citizenship, and democracy at the state level, while at the same time acknowledging our cosmopolitan obligations to recognize the rights of citizens in other states or without any state at all? I think so, and I will sketch this possibility in the next section.

The 'right to have rights': state citizenship and global justice

Citizenship provides the 'right to have rights' in two important senses. First, as we saw in the last chapter, membership of the citizen body gives access to the 'positive' or 'institutional' rights offered by a given political community. Second, as we remarked in Chapters 1 and 2, the exercise of political citizenship offers a means for claiming rights and shaping the ways they are conceived and implemented. Here, though, I want to explore the issues of whether this 'right' does not itself assume certain rights, and how far it is compatible with the recognition of the rights of those who are not co-citizens.

I noted when exploring the criteria for membership how participating as a political citizen assumes certain qualities and capacities – such as the ability to learn about and discuss public issues. To secure these opportunities for all implicitly involves providing citizens with rights to freedom of thought and speech, freedom of information, and possibly even a right to basic education. Likewise, even to cast a vote implies not just a right to vote but also freedom of association, regular elections, and so on. A common assumption stemming from this fact that the practices of democratic citizenship entail rights of various kinds is to argue that these rights must be preconditions for citizenship. As such, they deserve special protection within a domestic and possibly an international bill of rights and must even be protected from the operation of democratic citizenship itself. Indeed, some proponents of this view end up reading almost all conceivable rights as being somehow linked to the rights of democratic citizenship. Yet, by entrenching these rights in legally protected constitutions that are immune from political influence, this proposal paradoxically ends up subverting the actual exercise of democratic citizenship.

Therefore, though there is an element of truth in the argument that citizenship presupposes a set of pre-political rights, it is also somewhat topsy-turvy. After all, we observed in Chapter 2 how all these rights have been the products of citizenly activity. Moreover, it has been further political pressure that has progressively extended them to encompass new subjects – women as well as men, say; applied them to new spheres – not just the narrow political sphere but also the workplace, the family, and culture; refined their scope – so that rights are seen as rights to certain key goods, such as education, as well as rights against interference by governments and others; and broadened the style of rights legislation and adjudication to accommodate religious, cultural, and other differences. These ongoing political processes have been crucial for broadening and deepening rights and shaping them to accommodate the diversity and complexity of modern life. At the same time, they have altered what it is to be a political citizen – both who is a citizen, and how citizens can act within the political system and influence its decisions and form.

11. Martin Luther King before delivering his 'I have a dream' speech, 28 August 1963, from the steps of the Lincoln Memorial during the March on Washington for Jobs and Freedom, a defining moment of the American civil rights movement

So the rights that define citizenship also have to be seen as undergoing a continual process of redefinition through the political actions of citizens themselves: be it through their acting as voters or pressure groups to persuade politicians to pass new legislation, or by their bringing new cases before the courts. It is via such activities that citizens strive to improve the ways social and legal structures facilitate their freedom to pursue the goals and interests that give meaning to their lives on equal terms with others. They do so by seeking to obtain mutual recognition for the various relevant similarities and differences existing between themselves or their pursuits and those of others, so as to remove any unjust discrimination or disadvantages that may affect them. For example, it is through such action that women have won the right to maternity leave and gradually, if slowly, obtained limited support for child care at the workplace.

Even when political and other rights are enshrined in constitutional documents, they tend to undergo a process of reinterpretation in response to political pressure reflecting evolving social needs and views. However, change is generally slower than in countries, such as the United Kingdom, where such rights are simply enshrined in ordinary legislation. Of course, constitutional entrenchment may protect rights from being curtailed by politicians, either for their own convenience or in response to populist panics or prejudices, and can inspire popular movements to claim rights. The evidence for both these theoretical possibilities occurring in practice is mixed, though. As I remarked above, courts rarely deviate from sustained, national, majority opinion – they are part of the political system and naturally tend to reflect long-term trends within it. That said, raising the barrier to legislative change creates a bias in favour of the status quo that slows change. This tendency will naturally benefit the currently privileged over the underprivileged, for it will be the latter who seek reform. Whereas majoritarianism proves generally progressive, at least in culturally homogeneous societies, because it involves an implicit egalitarian and collective tendency – a point we explore more fully in the next chapter – the status quo bias leans towards the regressive and proves particularly so with respect to social and economic rights, which usually require redistribution from rich to poor. For example, historically it has greatly inhibited both labour legislation and health and welfare programmes in the United States compared to Western Europe.

Even when constitutional courts seek to protect minority groups, unless the rights concerned enjoy sufficient political recognition from citizens for governments to embody them in legislation and policy-making, little will change. Take the landmark decision of the US Supreme Court in *Brown v. Board of Education of Topeka*, 347 US 483 (1954). This case overturned a previous Court ruling in *Plessy v. Ferguson*, 163 US 537 (1896) that had deemed the segregation of black and white facilities in the southern states of America to be permissible so long as they were 'separate but equal' by declaring that 'separate educational facilities are inherently unequal'. As a result, racial segregation was now affirmed to be a violation of the Equal Protection Clause of the Fourteenth Amendment of the United States Constitution. Yet, ten years after this ruling no more than 1.2% of black children attended desegregated schools in the southern states. Change only began to occur as a result of the political actions of the African-American civil rights movement and the passage by Congress of the Civil Rights Act and the Voting Rights Act in 1964 and 1965. *Brown* may have helped energize support for such measures, but popular protest against racial discrimination would undoubtedly have arisen anyway. Meanwhile, the Court's decision also motivated a shift to the right by white southern politicians and staunch, and occasionally violent, opposition to reform. In any case, whatever its positive or negative effects, *Brown* failed to alter the material conditions of most African-Americans. Only getting a majority to pay for extensive social reforms will tackle the racial poverty gap within the United States.

At the global level, the courts are likely to be even more isolated from popular political influence, increasing the danger that they may incline more to the privileged with greater ease of access to them than the underprivileged. Of course, there are some transnational social and political movements, especially in such areas as the environment and poverty where concerted international action is needed. However, there are also much better funded lobbyists representing powerful commercial interests. Moreover, to have a real international impact, a transnational movement will still need to influence the domestic politics of numerous states because there is no world political authority to which they can appeal. Even organizations such as the United Nations or the European Union are largely intergovernmental in their operation. Nevertheless, though the international rights regimes have tended to disappoint many of their advocates, one should not be despondent. The very fact that states have created such bodies indicates that seeing citizenship and rights as primarily located within states need not be at variance with their promotion at the global level. Indeed, in a number of respects upholding citizenship as the right to have rights within one's own political community entails recognizing and supporting it for the citizens of other communities.

First, recognizing the state as the locus of the citizen's 'right to have rights' implies that states should endeavour to establish just terms of interaction between each other – that is, they should seek terms of global justice between states rather than all the individuals of the world, in which governments act as the representatives of their countries in much the same way as elected representatives act for their constituents. International agreements of these kinds serve a two-fold purpose. On the one hand, they endeavour to secure certain collective goods from which the citizens of all countries will benefit. On the other hand, they seek to guard against the activities of one country interfering with those of another in ways that might undermine the capacity of the citizens of the affected country from exercising their rights.

12. A meeting of the Council of the European Union in Brussels

Many agreements involve both these elements. So the collective good of peace is promoted by non-aggression pacts and collaboration in collective security arrangements. Likewise, action to protect the environment involves international agreements to collectively reduce emissions or regulate other activities, such as over-fishing depleted fish stocks. These sorts of agreements involve countries giving up short-term advantages for a long-term common benefit and are designed to prevent any one of them free-riding on the actions of others – for example, by continuing to pollute while other countries cut their emissions, thereby reaping the environmental advantages without paying any of the costs.

Such potential win-win settlements – which abound in the international sphere – are naturally easier to set up than those that involve wealthy countries losing long-term by giving up certain of their advantages *vis-à-vis* poorer states. Yet, on a range of issues, from bans on the exploitation of child labour or other oppressive work practices, to debt relief, slow but steady progress is being made. More generally, there is a growing sense that the terms of trade between countries should be equitable between rich and poor: for example, that the former should not be able to protect their own farmers while obliging the latter to import their agricultural products. These sorts of measures fall far short of the global redistribution of wealth advocated by some cosmopolitans, but over time have redistributive effects nonetheless. As I have remarked in earlier chapters, although non-exploitation and anti-discrimination are part of any welfare scheme, deepening this so as to offer positive aid to others involves additionally a sense of everyone playing fair by others and doing their bit. Scale alone militates against the development of the deeper solidarity and sense of reciprocity among citizens needed for a comprehensive welfare system operating across the globe. However, a commitment not to exploit others and hamper their efforts to create their own welfare systems can be seen as a strict requirement of justice for all states that is entailed by their own desire to develop such systems for their own citizens. Moreover, this scheme allows for variations in what a given state might offer. Citizens can tailor welfare to suit the political culture – prioritizing different elements, adopting alternative ways of funding, allowing diverse mixes of private and public provision, and so on.

Similar reasoning underpins a second aspect of the international dimension of the right to have rights: namely, that political communities should be granted rights to self-determination. This need not mean that every national, cultural, or ethnic group should have its own state – as we saw, the number of such groups greatly outstrips the likely number of viable states. It does suggest, though, that where a desire for self-government is voiced efforts should be made to devolve power or create power-sharing arrangements so long as in doing so an existing unit is not made less viable. It is a sign of a dictatorial regime that it seeks to suppress such demands, but that they are expressed the moment it collapses. For example, such has been the case in the former communist bloc of Central and Eastern Europe in the aftermath of 1989, and in Iraq post-Saddam Hussein. A parallel logic also implies that immigrants should not have discriminatory membership criteria applied to them. It is certainly in order that prospective citizens should show a degree of commitment to their chosen country, usually by a moderate residency requirement, and be able to operate as full members of their new country. But it is invidious to set the membership criteria higher than most existing citizens could attain – for example, by demanding a standard of literacy in the dominant language only achieved by the highly educated.

Finally, states and their citizens have a global obligation to uphold the humanitarian rights of citizens. In addition to the requirement to supply aid in crisis situations, discussed above, it also entails not sustaining regimes that oppress their citizens. Potentially, this obligation might support humanitarian intervention in the affairs of another state to prevent genocide and the mass murder of citizens. However, such actions must always be assessed on a case by case basis. Experience shows they can often backfire and produce an even worse situation. Often less drastic measures that simply curb a regime's ability to oppress offer a better, if far from ideal, solution. Upholding humanitarian rights through the prism of the right to have rights also presents states with a clear obligation to accept asylum seekers and to allow them to naturalize as citizens when either the prospects of their safely returning to their country of origin are remote, or they become established in their host country.

To summarize: a right to citizenship does imply certain rights, but these need not be such as to exhaust the whole concept of citizenship, as legal conceptions of citizenship propose. Rather, it is through being a citizen in a fuller, political sense that we generate rights. Although, for all practical purposes, the exercise of political citizenship is best pursued at the state level, this does not negate the notion of a global or cosmopolitan citizenship. Instead, it places an obligation on states and their citizens to secure the possibility for the exercise of citizenship within self-governing political communities for all. On the one hand, this duty involves not undermining the capacity of citizens in existing polities to govern themselves by exploiting or dominating their countries. On the other hand, it requires that non-citizens be allowed access to membership on non-discriminatory terms.

Chapter 5
Participation and democracy

We saw in Chapter 2 how for the ancient Greeks political participation formed an intrinsic part of citizenship. To enjoy the promise of civic equality that the status of citizenship holds out, all citizens had to play their part in the political process. Otherwise, instead of a situation of ruling and being ruled in turn, a citizen would simply be ruled. Indeed, our word 'idiot' comes from the Greek *idiotes*, a term used to describe someone who concentrated entirely on their private affairs to the neglect of the public realm. These days, though, most of us tend to be idiots in this respect.

Disenchantment with democratic politics has never been more pronounced, with voter turnout and trust in politicians in a slow but steady decline within all the established democracies. Political citizenship is rejected as both too demanding and of dubious worth. People increasingly adopt what I called the imperial Roman view of legal citizenship. They place their faith in the courts and other supposedly impartial, expert regulatory bodies to provide an equitable framework for their activities, rejecting politics as at best ineffective, at worst pernicious. I have already cast doubt on some of the assumptions underlying these kinds of arguments at various points throughout this book. This chapter seeks to make the case for linking citizenship and democratic politics in a more systematic fashion. In particular, I want to argue that democratic politics as it is practised in the established democracies, such as the United States, Britain, Sweden, Germany, New Zealand, Australia, or Canada, does not deserve anything like the cynicism and criticism that it has become conventional to direct at it.

In Chapter 2 we noted that, like many of the political terms examined so far, the word 'democracy' has Greek roots, literally meaning 'people' (*demos*) 'rule' (*kratos*). We also saw, in Chapter 3, that who the 'people' are begs a number of questions that can be answered in various ways – from the very narrow in scope, as was the case in ancient Greece where women and slaves, among others, were excluded, to the very broad, on certain cosmopolitan accounts encompassing the whole of humanity. Much the same applies to the nature and sense in which the people, however defined, are said to 'rule'. What 'rule' involves can also be read in narrower or broader terms. On the broadest accounts, democratic rule involves all the relevant people taking every collective decision by consensus. On the narrowest of accounts, it suggests that rulers should simply rule for the benefit of all the people – whether or not they happen to be chosen from or by the people: a hereditary line of enlightened despots would be 'democratic' in this sense so long as their rule was benevolent and beneficial. Midway between these two positions lie the actually existing democratic systems of today, whereby democratic rule means that rulers are to some degree chosen by, accountable to, and removable by, the ruled.

Much of the criticism of what might be called 'real' or 'actual' democracy stems from comparisons with the imagined superiority of the supposedly 'ideal' democracy offered by either the broad account of direct participatory democratic rule, whereby all are involved in making and administering the law, or the narrow account's vision of a class of benevolent expert rulers who, free from prejudice or private interest, have the ability and desire to govern for the people rather than themselves. The first section points out some problems with both these alternatives. It turns out that neither captures the idea of a political community of equals that lies at the heart of citizenship. I shall offer an alternative account of democracy that is more in tune with this idea, exploring in the second section how far contemporary democratic practices serve to realize it. Finally, the third section concludes this chapter and the book as a whole with some reflections on the prospects for political citizenship in contemporary societies.

What is democracy, and why is it important for citizenship?

This section will explore 'direct' or 'participatory' democracy, in which all citizens participate in law-making, and guardianship, where no participation is involved. In pointing out the problems of both, I hope to highlight the merits of the real systems of representative democracy that characterize most working democracies today.

Participatory democracy

The 18th-century French philosopher Jean-Jacques Rousseau – the last great advocate of the ancient model of participatory citizenship – famously declared that the 'people of England' were 'free only during the election of members of parliament. As soon as they are elected, slavery overtakes it, and it is nothing.' Many contemporary critics of today's democracies are apt to go even further and complain that even when electing the legislature, the people are not ruling – at best they are voting for their rulers from among a pre-selected shortlist that offers them little in the way of choice. I shall explore the accuracy of this characterization of democratic elections below. But what of the implied alternative?

At its most extreme, a radical democratic position becomes almost synonymous with anarchism. According to this view, people can rule themselves democratically only if they take every decision, can weigh up all alternatives, and come to a unanimous conclusion. Otherwise, the minority in any vote will be ruled by the majority rather than ruling themselves. Yet it does not take much thought to see how difficult this result would be to achieve in practice. Imagine that an election involves four main issues: inheritance tax, spending on hospitals, the terms of an international treaty, and involvement in a military campaign on foreign soil. Suppose, then, there are 3 possible policies being canvassed on the first issue, 5 on the second, 4 on the third, and 2 on the last. That gives $3 \times 5 \times 4 \times 2 = 120$ possible views that a citizen might take on these issues. To vote on all of them would be time-consuming enough, to expect unanimity – even after a long, public-spirited discussion of the merits of each of them – not only raises the degree of commitment expected of each citizen to a level that starts to exclude having time for anything else, but also is highly unlikely given that each policy option is liable to reflect different and occasionally incompatible moral positions and empirical assumptions which can all claim a reasonable degree of plausibility. Given that my example considerably simplifies the number and complexity of the issues and related policy options that generally need to be decided by governments in advanced societies, the prospects of direct participatory government seem remote, to say the least. Even if we drop the unanimity condition, it will simply be too time-consuming and inefficient to involve everyone in debating and deciding every single issue. It would raise the transaction costs of each decision to a level where government would grind to a halt.

It is sometimes suggested we could reserve such methods for the absolutely key issues, such as constitutional amendments, and those that affect us most closely – notably the very local or those in the workplace. Both proposals are certainly more plausible from a practical perspective. However, each invokes a slightly different line of argument for more direct democracy, with the reasoning underlying the second proposal proving more convincing than the reasons supporting the first. The rationale for having referenda on constitutional issues is often said to be that although it is impractical and perhaps unnecessary for people to decide all policy questions collectively, they could only be said to rule

13. French campaign posters for the referendum on the European Constitution, 29 May 2005

themselves so long as the 'rules' by which they are ruled are directly and collectively made.

Yet, for a constitutional referendum fully to live up to these expectations, it too would need to involve both the opportunity of voting on all the possible options, otherwise voters have at best only a negative voice to reject proposals advanced by others, and be repeated at regular intervals, otherwise past voters – many, possibly all, if one thinks for example of the US Constitution, dead – will be effectively binding present voters. These stipulations might be said to be made unnecessary so long as amendments are possible. However, if changes need unanimity or, as is more common, a supermajority of voters to be passed (that is, more than 50% – with two-thirds of the electorate being a regular condition), then a 'status quo' bias is established. In practice, additional votes are awarded to what exists, because far more are required for change than for things to stay as they are. That may seem appropriate if one can assume that what exists is likely to be superior to any proposed reform. But there is no sound reason to believe this to be the case. On the contrary, unless all citizens are entirely equitably and fairly situated at the time a given constitution is enacted, a condition so far never met anywhere, then there is a real danger entrenchment will merely further advantage the privileged against the underprivileged. Moreover, it is very hard to anticipate the potential perverse effects of particular clauses or the ways societies may change. For example, many provisions of the US Constitution clearly reflect the time-bound assumptions of 18th-century America, when militias provided the role now allotted to a professional army and news travelled only as fast as the fastest horse. However, although a majority might well wish to change these and other clauses, doing so has proven extremely difficult because those who gain advantage from them can hold out against reform.

Many of these criticisms were made somewhat presciently by Thomas Jefferson in letters to one of the drafters and key proponents of the American Constitution, James Madison. As Madison came to appreciate, they point not just to practical but also logical and normative problems with seeing democracy as a system of collective self-rule. Although a given people may regard themselves as having collective problems that require a common solution, the degree to which they identify themselves as a collectivity will always be limited. Despite sharing certain values and concerns, they may make divergent empirical and moral assessments as to the advisability of certain policies and their conduciveness to the public interest. They may also have equally reasonable but incompatible interests or commitments. As a result, any collective policy will require a degree of give and take from people, with some almost inevitably compromising more than others. Consequently, almost all involved in any collective decision will be to some degree ruled by others. So, the electorate of a country may agree we need a collective policy to tackle the threats posed by global warming. But for a whole host of reasons – from ideological differences, to differing interests and evaluations of the scientific evidence – they may disagree as to what precisely ought to be done. Among the package of measures any government is likely to adopt, most people will find some they agree with and others they do not. So John may agree and Paul disagree with the increased use of sources of alternative energy, such as wind power, but John disagree and Paul agree with raising fuel taxes. Both John and Paul may support the government, but John rules Paul on the first measure and Paul rules John on the second.

Treating democracy as a system of popular sovereignty, in which people rule themselves, proves misleading, therefore. Moreover, it directs attention away from, and may even undermine, its true role as a fair decision-making process among political equals. Seen in this light, the core purpose of democracy can be aligned directly with the underlying rationale of citizenship given in this book – namely, the establishment of a condition of civic equity. As we noted in Chapter 1, citizenship assumes both social relations and, by contrast to anarchism, the necessity of the state to regulate them. Its importance arises precisely because our freedom as individuals can be both limited by the freedom of others and require their active cooperation, producing a need for collective rules and policies that mediate our potential conflicts and promote valuable public goods. Citizenship is about ensuring these rules and policies treat all those involved as deserving equal concern and respect. Regarding democracy as a system of self-rule denies the very need for such common structures because it suggests we all ought to be able somehow to get what we want – that it would be 'undemocratic' for John and Paul, in my example above, to compromise at all. Worse, it potentially subverts the search for equitable solutions by allowing individuals to hold out against any changes that might threaten their existing privileges. By contrast, a more citizenship-centred view of the democracy regards it as a fair process whereby we settle our differences and pursue our collective ends on an equal basis – accepting that of necessity this involves ruling and being ruled in turn.

When we turn to the second proposal I gave above of where more direct and participatory forms of democratic politics might be plausibly employed – namely, when making very local decisions among a relatively small group of people, such as in neighbourhood associations or the workplace – then it is in fact their link to political equality that gives them their best rationale. The smallness of the group means all can have a say and an opportunity to listen and respond to others, and so are more likely mutually to adjust their positions to reflect their respective arguments and concerns. Moreover, because they live nearby or work together, they usually have a number of fairly well-defined shared purposes and issues, and so identify themselves as more of a collectivity. As a result, the areas and principles over which they might disagree and the range of options they need to consider will be much more circumscribed than within a larger, more heterogeneous community. Even so, consensus may not be possible or even desirable given that, as we saw above, it may simply be a way for the prejudiced or privileged to hold out against legitimate change. Consequently, a decision may need to be made by majority vote. Yet, nobody need feel too excluded as a result – each has had a hearing and been able to vote on the same terms as everyone else.

In these local settings, therefore, participation and direct democracy will often support political equality because they allow all views to be given a full and equal airing, and enable citizens to take on board the opinions and preferences of others. By contrast, note how direct involvement in a referendum – which is often upheld as a model of ideal, direct democracy – gives no opportunity for voters to mutually modify their positions to show equal respect for the views of others. And, as we saw, if the vote requires more than a majority to be passed, as is often the case, then those who favour change are treated less equally than those who prefer the status quo. As such, it fails by the standard of citizenship by not encouraging participants to view each other as equals.

Guardianship

What of the other ideal of democracy canvassed above, that of decision-making by benevolent experts? Advocates of this argument contend that rule *by* the people often fails to deliver rule *for* the people – not least because giving equal weight to all views offers no guarantee that outcomes will be either equitable or serve the public interest. Instead, they are more likely to reflect ignorant or self-serving prejudices. These dangers can be corrected by either the objectivity offered by expertise, or the impartiality provided by a neutral 'third' party. As a result, citizens will often be better off not participating in ruling themselves and trusting instead in specially selected guardians. Yet each of the claims underlying this proposal is suspect.

The argument based on the objectivity of expertise originated with Plato. He maintained that democracy was analogous to handing the running of a ship to the passengers rather than entrusting it to a captain. Just as handling tides and rough seas and keeping the ship from being dashed to pieces on the rocks was a job for a trained professional, so, he reasoned, government was likewise a matter for those who had the capacity for and had learned the art of governing. The difficulty is that this analogy breaks down at a number of places. First, there is no 'objective' science of either the ends that governments should pursue, or necessarily of the best means to realize them. Both are subject to often contentious and fallible judgements. Human reasoning has proven incapable of defining with certainty the most appropriate course of action in all circumstances for all human beings. The openness of the social world, the fact that human beings operate in unpredictable and multifarious ways, make social science far less 'hard' than either natural science or mathematics, where reasoning operates within an empirically and logically closed set of parameters according to common norms. Consequently, though the captain may deal with the technicalities of sailing the ship, it is the passengers who rightly determine its destination. For there is no science of best destinations for all people apart from what they themselves see as most suitable given what they seek out of life.

Second, unless we assume experts to be unfailingly selfless and altruistic as well as omniscient, there is no guarantee that they will rule for the benefit of others rather than themselves. Though experts design and build the ship and a captain charts its course, it is not their benevolence but the need to woo passengers that leads them to respond in a variety of ways to what people want and in the process improve both ship design and navigation. Without that incentive, many technical improvements – especially those specifically 'for' the people – might never come about. Of course, competition between sea captains and their companies takes place in the market, and although the terms may be equal for all, not all passengers have equal standing – the wealthy are better positioned than the poor. Yet, those issues that should be the same for all regardless of wealth, such as basic matters relating to the sea-worthiness of the vessel, the qualifications of captains, and so on, arise from state legislation that responds to the more substantive equality provided by democratic voting. Again, these are technical issues, and politicians will necessarily draw on the advice of a whole range of expert advice when formulating legislation on such matters. But governments take them into account because citizens have pressurized them to respond to sea disasters and the like by imposing a basic regulatory structure on the shipping industry that reflects matters of public interest that market competition alone would be unlikely to secure on an equal basis for all. Meanwhile, most technical solutions will raise problematic empirical and moral issues that even experts may disagree upon. For example, there will be a balance to be made between safety and various costs of time, the price of a ticket, and so on. Again, the most appropriate judges of the risks involved will be those likely to bear them and in a position to weigh them against their other concerns and interests – namely, citizens.

Plato's case for 'objective' rule by experts rests on dubious foundations, therefore. It fails to displace the democratic case that the best guide we have that social and political decisions will be in the public interest is that they reflect the expressed and evolving choices of citizens under conditions of political equality, and that rulers are accountable to them for their actions. The impartiality argument also has Greek roots but takes a slightly different tack. The claim here is that citizens are likely to be partial to their own concerns and so fail to accord equal concern and respect to those of others. As a result, we may need an impartial arbitrator to ensure all views are considered fairly. That need not be a guarantee the right decision is reached, but at least it will not result from bias or prejudice.

A key difficulty with this proposal is whether such an impartial arbitrator exists. Judges are often portrayed in this guise, and in certain circumstances they can be – for example, when adjudicating domestic disputes between separating couples. However, when deciding collective decisions affecting all citizens, they are as much a party to any disagreements as anyone else. Of course, their declared reasoning is constrained by points of law – yet this may be a hindrance rather than an advantage to the extent that it forecloses giving a full consideration of the complete range of moral and empirical issues raised by a given case.

Moreover, the dangers of partiality among the electorate are overdrawn. The fear here is of the tyranny of the majority. Yet, it is necessary to specify carefully when a majority could be said to be tyrannous. This is likely to occur in cases when the majority who decide is identical to that whose rights and interests are at stake in the decision. The commonest example of this phenomenon is when an ethnic group votes to boost its own privileges at the expense of another ethnic group, as occurred in the past in Northern Ireland, where the Protestant majority consistently boosted their own position with respect to the Catholic minority. However, these are special cases which, as in Northern Ireland, can be accommodated through democratic mechanisms that force power-sharing between the main groups. It is unclear that issues such as affirmative action or abortion, to cite two key areas of judicial decision-making in the United States and elsewhere, conform to this pattern. On these sorts of issues, judges are as partisan as every other citizen in that they have a personal view of the matter. Meanwhile, those most affected – minority groups and women respectively – are as divided in their views of these policies as the rest of the population. It is not that all white males vote against them and all black women for them.

What democracy provides in this instance is an impartial process for resolving the dispute. 'One person, one vote' recognizes each citizen as equally entitled to have their view given as much weight as anybody else's. Of course, equal weighting in the decision-making process offers no guarantee that the decision itself will be one that treats all with equal concern and respect. Yet the very fact that majorities usually have to be constructed by winning the support of millions of citizens, with most citizens finding themselves in a minority on some issues and a majority on others, creates an egalitarian bias within democracy. Because everyone is involved in making all decisions, there is an incentive on the part of citizens to give equal consideration to the views of others for fear that they will not receive it themselves. Many readers may feel this is a somewhat idealized view of the democratic process. In the next section, therefore, I want to show how many features of existing democratic systems actually promote this result.

Citizenship and democracy today

The political systems of those countries we call democracies could not be more different from the model of direct, participatory democracy, though they increasingly involve many elements of supposed democratic guardianship. Their main democratic features lie in offering regular elections in which all adults can select between the representatives of competing parties by some form of majority vote. All these elements have been criticized by proponents of the two democratic ideals explored in the last section for either failing to engage citizens fully in the democratic process, or encouraging populism and pandering to the lowest common denominator. But each of them makes an important contribution towards securing political equality between citizens in ways that are appropriate to contemporary conditions. In particular, they promote the three qualities we saw these two alternatives lacked: first, equity in the formulation of collective decisions; second, the accountability of rulers to the ruled and incentives for them to pursue the public's interest rather their own; and third, impartiality in the resolving of disagreements.

Strictly speaking, a system of majority rule involves making decisions according to one person, one vote and going with those options that receive more than 50% of the votes cast. From the perspective of political equality, this arrangement has the benefit of treating all people's views in an anonymous and neutral manner – it does not matter who you are or what you believe or why, your judgement counts exactly the same as everyone else's. It also reflects shifts in opinion, so that if the people's views move from 60% against a motion to 49% against and 51% in favour, then the decision passes. In consequence, it accords all views equal respect. Nevertheless, there are a number of possible problems.

For a start, not all democracies employ a genuine system of majority rule. Notoriously, Britain and the United States use an electoral system whereby a party need only attract more votes than any other in a majority of the legislative constituencies to win an election. Technically speaking, these are plurality systems and consistent with the winning party not only attracting fewer than 50% of votes cast – a frequent occurrence in both countries – but also fewer votes than the runner-up, although so far this has happened only three times in Britain – in 1951, when Labour polled more votes but the Conservatives gained more parliamentary seats, and in 1929 and the first election of 1974, when, by a narrower margin, the reverse occurred.

The various forms of proportional representation (PR) seek to overcome this problem but run into difficulties of their own when electors are offered more than two options. PR systems look at how voters rank their preferences among all the available options and select the one that most people rank highest. These systems certainly offer a more equitable mechanism for weighing votes than the plurality, first past the post, mechanism adopted in the USA and UK. However, the different forms of proportional representation aggregate people's preferences in different ways and so identify different options as the most highly preferred. Worse, it may well be that if we compared people's ranking of each option against that of every other option, we would find that none of them was uniquely preferred over all others.

Take the following simple example of 100 voters choosing which of three sources of generating electricity to support:

40 Voters	30 Voters	30 Voters
Nuclear Power	Coal	Wind Energy
Wind Energy	Nuclear Energy	Coal
Coal	Wind Energy	Nuclear Power

As we can see, 70 voters prefer nuclear power to wind energy, while 70 voters prefer wind energy to coal, but 60 voters prefer coal to nuclear energy. So no single option is uniquely preferred over all others. This phenomenon is known as a voting cycle and was first identified by the Marquis of Condorcet in the 18th century, and then rediscovered by Charles Dodgson – the mathematician better known as Lewis Carol, the author of *Alice in Wonderland*. In the event of such cycles, selecting any option as more preferred than any other seems arbitrary. It will be a function of the voting system and the ways politicians manipulate it.

Fortunately, though logically possible, these sorts of dilemmas turn out to be rare in practice. One reason for this rarity stems from the role of parties. Parties bring together people's different preferences on a whole range of issues into a single programme, uniting them within an overall ideological framework along a spectrum that in most democracies goes from left to right. That simplifies the actual choice voters have to make to something more like a decision between two alternatives. Even within a multi-party system, they are generally choosing along a continuum of left to right. In competing for people's votes during elections, parties have an incentive to build, or in a multi-party system to be part of, a winning coalition. So they try and develop or form part of a package of policies that will reflect people's most preferred ranking on different issues. They achieve this result by converging on the median voter – that is, the voter whose preference rankings are at the mid-point between the two extremes. That convergence is sometimes mistakenly criticized for failing to give voters a choice. However, the opposite turns out to be the case – it is actually the result of parties seeking to maximize the degree to which they reflect voter choice. In effect, electoral campaigns mirror the results of deliberation in small settings. In formulating and discussing the most electorally attractive policy packages, parties are essentially coordinating the mutual accommodation of millions of citizens' views and preoccupations so that they align with their most favoured preference orderings. As a result, voters' views are not only equally respected, but are likely to be shown equal concern too.

Meanwhile, party discipline keeps representatives to their electoral pledges. An aspect of the participatory critique of representative government voiced by Rousseau and others is that once elected representatives are free to do as they please. Indeed, prior to the full development of parties, the electoral process was often characterized as the means whereby the electorate selected the most able rulers from among their social or intellectual betters rather than a mechanism for influencing policy. In essence, it amounted to an electoral form of guardianship. This view was most famously expressed by the 18th-century English statesman and philosopher Edmund Burke when he informed the electors of Bristol that 'your representative owes you, not his industry only, but his judgement; and he betrays, instead of serving you, if he sacrifices it to your opinion'. However, contemporary parties remain remarkably faithful to their electoral commitments. Though the tendency of parties to force their representatives to vote on block is often criticized on Burkean grounds by media commentators, it is in fact essential for their accountability to the judgements of the electorate. Of course, unanticipated issues and circumstances arise that call for changes in the legislative programme, but these tend to be made within the framework set by the last election or, more frequently perhaps, in anticipation of the next.

Somewhat oddly from a democratic perspective, this attentiveness of politicians to the views of the electorate is occasionally criticized as revealing how they will do anything for power. Yet that criticism is as nonsensical as attacking commercial firms for pandering to the wishes of customers simply to make a profit. Just as markets exploit the entrepreneur's desire for a profit to the customers' advantage by using competition to prompt them to innovate and lower costs so as to maintain or increase their market share, so democratic systems employ electoral competition for the benefit of voters by harnessing the desire of politicians for power and their fear of losing it to make them responsive to policy failures and the evolving views of the ruled.

Moreover, politicians no more do 'anything' for power than most entrepreneurs pursue profit at all costs. In particular, politicians and their parties remain remarkably faithful to their 'brand' or ideology. Even when stealing the opposition's policies – itself a benefit to voters in that it reflects the need to build coalitions across the party divide – they attempt to do so in ways that are consistent with an evolving ideological identity. Political cynicism proves much rarer than journalists tend to make out.

These effects are all good news for citizens. At the small cost of a reasonably low input from them, they can get governments to address their interests and views in ways that treat them – via the voting system – with a high degree of equal concern and respect. They can remove unresponsive or incompetent politicians and arrive at collective decisions in an impartial manner. Yet, it is undeniable that disaffection for the workings of democracy has never been higher. Why has this dissatisfaction arisen, and what does it tell us about the nature of citizenship today?

14. **Barack Obama campaigning to be the Democratic Party's presidential candidate, 2008**

The end of citizenship?

As we have seen, citizenship involves a degree of solidarity and reciprocity between citizens. They need to see each other as equal partners within a collective enterprise in which they share the costs as well as the benefits. That holds as much for participating in elections as paying taxes. For various reasons, such sentiments seem to be on the decline. Two broad and, in certain respects, related manifestations of this phenomenon stand out: the growth of a more consumer-orientated attitude towards the state and government, and the fragmentation and attenuation of political community.

Voting within modern democratic systems is sometimes portrayed and criticized for being self-interested. Indeed, this view often lies behind fears of tyrannous majorities. As I noted in Chapter 1, though, the self-interested voter would be more inclined to stay at home. The probability that any one person's vote would make a difference is so small, that the costs of time and inconvenience will almost certainly outweigh any expected benefit. To vote, individuals must feel it is important to express their views within the public arena, and that their voice connects in various ways with the voices of millions of others, so that it is not just an isolated vote that they are casting. For rather different reasons, certain groups of people have started abandoning this civic duty.

One group, characterized by the economist J. K. Galbraith as the affluent 'contented majority', have become more ambivalent about electoral politics as they have grown increasingly unwilling to contribute to collective goods from which they may only benefit indirectly. They seek a more direct correlation, akin to that enjoyed by customers in the market, between what they pay and what they get as individuals. In consequence, they are inclined to accept a gradual privatization of many hitherto public services, such as health, education, and even the police. Privatization undermines civic attitudes not so much through private suppliers providing public goods and services, which in certain cases may produce gains in terms of efficiency compared to a state-run provider, as when such goods become perceived as private consumables rather than a collective responsibility, that ought by right to be supplied to all citizens on an equitable basis. If a family has private health insurance and does not use the public education system, they will be less inclined to support their provision at public expense for others. This group's political activity takes a correspondingly more privatized form. They gravitate towards narrower campaigns and pressure groups, often focused on a single issue, deserting the more encompassing representation offered by parties. They seek consumer rights and privileges with regard to particular public services, but are unprepared to pay for the improvements through higher taxes.

This shift in the social attitudes and political activity of the more affluent citizens is connected to one aspect of the fragmentation of modern communities produced by the growing gap between rich and poor over the past 30 years. These two groups have gradually come to inhabit different worlds, with the former tempted to see the latter as a problem to be contained rather than as fellow citizens within a shared system of social cooperation. Meanwhile, the social exclusion of the poor includes difficulties in organizing politically and comparatively lower levels of participation. Parties find themselves caught in a dilemma as a result. If they seek to ape the changes in the electorate and become more like single issue campaigning groups, they attract criticism for cynically departing from their role as inclusive and principled movements aiming at the collective good. Yet, if they adopt that traditional strategy, they risk losing affluent voters without attracting the votes of the poor.

Cultural fragmentation poses a parallel problem. Attention in the media tends to focus on multiculturalism resulting from immigration. However, we saw in Chapter 3 how by and large immigrants seek inclusion within the wider political community through policies of non-discrimination. The aim of the vast majority of immigrants has been to broaden the political culture of the host state by removing its discriminatory elements, not to create political enclaves to preserve a culture that most second- and third-generation immigrants come to merge with, or even discard for, that of the host state. By contrast, already existing, territorially concentrated minority nations and ethnic groups have become ever more vocal in their demands for greater political autonomy, especially when accompanied by religious and linguistic differences from the dominant national group. These demands have led to the asymmetric devolution of power to those territories controlled by given minorities, such as Wales, Scotland, and Northern Ireland in Britain, or Quebec in Canada, and in Catalonia and the Basque region in Spain.

What the growing divide between rich and poor, and the cultural split between minority nations or ethnicities and the majority national political culture, share in common is that both represent developing segmental or vertical divisions within contemporary societies. Democracy works best when the main disagreements among the population are cross-cutting or horizontal divisions. In these cases, politically important divisions cross over each other. So there will be socialists among the rich and conservatives among the poor, there will be poor and rich Catholics who oppose abortion, and poor and rich people who are pro-choice, there will be men and women who favour and oppose affirmative action, and in both cases some will be black and others white, with rich and poor and those pro- and anti-abortion on each side, and so on.

As a result, consistent minorities are likely to be rare – that is, people who are in a minority on every issue they care about. The anti-abortionist may be in a minority on that issue, but could be in the majority on affirmative action, say. Of course, the issue they care the most about may be the one they are in a minority on, but the 'intensity' of that situation is likely to be mitigated by their getting their way on many other (for them) lesser issues. Such balancing occurs as much within as between parties – especially in predominantly two-party systems. The resulting need for everyone to compromise is often misguidedly denigrated as unprincipled. However, it is precisely this need that produces toleration and mutual recognition between citizens, enabling all to be seen as equals and to some degree be included within any winning majority. Even when one's most favoured party is in opposition, at least some of one's preferences are likely to be adopted by the governing party, and possibly promoted better by them than one's own preferred party.

When vertical divisions predominate, such inclusiveness is harder to achieve. Although many cross-cutting issues may exist, the prime identity will be ethnicity, religion, or nationality and all other issues will be subordinated to it. In Belgium, for example, there are Flemish- and French-speaking conservative and socialist parties, but their collaboration is mitigated by the predominance of the cultural and linguistic divide.

In such cases, voting rarely influences the policy choices of governments because its main purpose is to obtain influence for one's cultural group. Here the danger of minority oppression is greater because of the separation between the two groups. Power-sharing may overcome this danger to a degree but can be at the expense of democratic responsiveness. In Belgium, for example, elections now barely reflect the issue of how the people are governed, just the extent to which one's group is involved in the governing coalition, be that government effective or not. If divisions become too entrenched, then the only solution may be complete separation. Yet the vast majority of states will contain some significant cultural minorities, so there will always be limits as to how far this strategy can be taken. The parallel with the divide between rich and poor is that the former likewise secede from the broader political community into their own gated communities. They withdraw from contributing to the public sector and seek to rely on private service providers alone.

Globalization has further dissipated political community. States become weaker and less able to deliver collective goods, increasing consumerist and privatized political action. National political cultures are similarly weakened by global market pressures to greater mobility and the enhanced ability to defect from collaborative arrangements. We noted in Chapter 4 how this

15. The Flemish nationalist group Voorpost carrying a symbolic coffin of Belgium

development has been welcomed by cosmopolitans, who see the potential for a post-national culture that overcomes cultural, socio-economic, and political divisions through a commitment to human rights. As the European Union, without doubt the most developed transnational political community in the world, reveals, though, such hopes seem far from realized. The EU's political organization remains firmly based in the national and subnational allegiances of citizens, with European parties mere parliamentary factions with no electoral presence. Meanwhile, the EU's *raison d'être* has been to enhance the free movement of capital, goods, labour, and services in order to promote a European-wide market. While beneficial economically, this policy has fostered the forces weakening national political communities without creating a European political culture. Participation in EU elections is even lower and falling faster than in domestic politics, though privileged groups have exploited to great effect the more privatized routes of pressure group politics and legal action.

What is to be done? Two of the most canvassed solutions are more participatory forms of democracy, either through referenda or among selected affected interests or focus groups, such as citizens' juries, and various forms of expert guardianship. These have been increasingly deployed as supplements, and even alternatives, to electoral democracy within well-established democratic systems, such as the UK and the USA, as well as being extensively used in the EU, where (as we noted) it has proved impossible to create a genuine *demos* or party democracy. Tasks hitherto undertaken by the elected administration in these countries have increasingly been devolved onto unelected and semi-independent regulators – be it the setting of interest rates by the governor of a central bank, the determination of the minimum wage by special commissions, or the arbitration of disputes about the location of nuclear reactors by judicial tribunals.

To the extent that citizens have any say at all in such matters, it is through consultation exercises via deliberative juries among a representative sample of the public, the involvement of campaigning groups; or local and, very occasionally, national referenda. However, we saw that these devices are more part of the problem than its solution, for each works against the idea of a condition of civic equality which is the defining feature of citizenship. Deference to expertise suggests that the issue is one that citizens are either incompetent or untrustworthy to express an opinion on, or that is somehow beyond politics – a matter of how things are. Either way, such moves suggest that it is somehow unnecessary and even illegitimate for citizens to seek to engage with each other as equals in deliberating about matters of collective concern. As such, it reinforces the disenchantment with and withdrawal from politics as a civic duty to reach agreement on the public good. That is not helped by consultation exercises with selected citizens and groups. For, as we saw, these likewise do not encourage citizens to accommodate and respond to the needs and views of others when framing collective policies. On the contrary, they allow citizens to employ politics to pursue purely private concerns or voice personal beliefs without any requirement to take account of the opinions of their fellow citizens.

Attempts to rebuild a commitment to political participation through citizenship education represent a more promising response, although as we saw in Chapter 3, they are not without problems of their own. By and large, patterns of civic engagement or disengagement are created at an early age. Studies have shown that voting or not voting in the very first election for which one is eligible is a good guide to one's likely participation or lack of it in later life. So, the more young people can be informed about and interested in democratic politics prior to their first opportunity to vote, the better. Civic engagement is also likely to be improved by attempts to devolve power to more local communities. Shared values and common purposes are likely to be stronger in such settings, and with them the willingness to engage in collective programmes.

However, the biggest nettle to grasp is probably that of widening social and economic inequality. As we have seen, more than anything else it is the capacity for the wealthy to remove themselves from collective arrangements that erodes the commitment to a search for public solutions on the basis of political equality. Globalization is often blamed for this development, with the dominance of market forces said to be inevitable when companies can operate outside state control by organizing production and exchange transnationally. Yet, such arguments appear to be exaggerated. As the example of the Scandinavian countries shows, it remains entirely possible for states to adapt to this new global economic environment and compete successfully, while retaining a commitment to their traditionally high levels of welfare and social spending. Moreover, through cooperation in regional bodies such as the EU, they have been able collectively to regulate global economic processes.

Commentators tend to divide as to whether they blame the current decline in active political citizenship on citizens themselves, social forces, such as globalization, or politicians and political structures. No doubt all share some responsibility. However, as we have seen, none can be regarded as being beyond remedy or as having rendered the ideal of citizenship either implausible or incoherent. Nation states retain their capacity, both alone and increasingly through cooperation, to tackle the economic, social, and cultural problems of today's globalized and complex societies. They also remain a highly suitable context for what remains the most appealing and viable form of democratic politics: namely, a system of representative democracy based on competing political parties.

Above all, the appeal of a society of civic equals who share in fashioning their collective life remains a powerful one. Citizenship informs and gives effect to central features of our social morality. It underlies our whole sense of self-worth, affecting in the process the ways we treat others and are treated by them. It stands behind the commitment to rights and the appreciation of cultural diversity that are among the central moral achievements of the late 20th and early 21st centuries. It has become fashionable to try and detach these effects of citizenship from any involvement in politics or democracy. What I hope to have shown in this book is that that is not possible. Citizenship and democratic politics stand and fall together. To seek to divorce the two undermines not just the possibility of political citizenship, but the values associated with the very idea of citizenship itself. The reinvigoration of citizenship, therefore, depends on revitalizing rather than diminishing political participation and with it the sense of belonging and the commitment to rights that are its prime benefits.

Further reading

General reading

There are several general books and collections of essays available for those who want to explore the themes of this book further. Most of them combine some treatment of the history of citizenship with a discussion of contemporary issues.

P. B. Clarke, *Citizenship* (Pluto Press, 1994) and H. R. van Gunsteren, *A Theory of Citizenship: Organising Plurality in Contemporary Democracies* (Westview, 1998) attempt respectively to update the Greek and Roman accounts of citizenship outlined in Chapter 2.

J. M. Barbalet, *Citizenship: Rights, Struggle and Class Inequality* (Open University Press, 1988); T. Janoski, *Citizenship and Civil Society* (Cambridge University Press, 1998); and B. Turner, *Citizenship and Capitalism: The Debate over Reformism* (Unwin Hyman, 1986) develop in different ways the sociological themes also discussed in Chapter 2.

Two useful collections of essays covering the whole field are R. Beiner (ed.), *Theorizing Citizenship* (SUNY Press, 1995), and E. F. Isin and B. S. Turner, *Handbook of Citizenship Studies* (Sage, 2003).

Chapter 1

The general books mentioned above all address the issues discussed here and attempt to come up with a definition of citizenship suited to modern conditions.

D. Heater, *What Is Citizenship?* (Polity, 1998) covers much the same themes but offers in many respects a contrasting, less political, account of citizenship to the one presented in this book. P. Norris (ed.), *Critical Citizens* (Oxford University Press, 1999) provides a useful collection of essays on changing patterns of political participation in the world's main democracies.

Chapter 2

The essay by J. G. A. Pocock, 'The Ideal of Citizenship since Classical Times', can be found in R. Beiner (ed.), *Theorizing Citizenship* (SUNY Press, 1995), pp. 29–52. M. Walzer's 'Citizenship' appears in T. Ball, J. Farr, and R. L. Hanson, *Political Innovation and Conceptual Change* (Cambridge University Press, 1989), pp. 211–19. T. H. Marshall's classic essay was published as *Citizenship and Social Class* (Cambridge University Press, 1950).

D. Heater, *A Brief History of Citizenship* (Edinburgh University Press, 2004) and P. Magnette, *Citizenship: The History of an Idea* (ECPR Press, 2005) both offer accessible histories of the concept. M. Mann, 'Ruling Strategies and Citizenship', *Sociology*, 21 (1987), pp. 339–54 is an influential critique of T. H. Marshall, while D. Held, *Political Theory and the Modern State* (Polity, 1989), chapter 7 offers a defence. R. Bellamy, D. Castiglione, and E. Santoro (eds), *Lineages of European Citizenship: Rights, Belonging and Citizenship in Eleven Nation-States* (Palgrave, 2004) explores the development of citizenship in Europe, with a chapter on the United States for comparative purposes, a topic dealt with at book length in J. N. Shklar, *American Citizenship: The Quest for Inclusion* (Harvard University Press, 1998).

Chapter 3

As the subtitle of Shklar's book indicates, issues of membership, inclusion, and exclusion form a central theme of the historical accounts listed in Chapter 2. The impact of women's membership of the citizenship body is discussed in R. Lister, *Citizenship: Feminist Perspectives*, 2nd edn. (Palgrave, 2003) and B. Siim, *Gender and Citizenship* (Cambridge University Press, 2000). Multiculturalism and ethnic diversity are discussed in W. Kymlicka, *Multicultural Citizenship* (Clarendon Press, 1995), and W. Kymlicka and W. Norman (eds), *Citizenship in Diverse Societies* (Oxford University Press, 2000). The link between nationality and citizenship is explored in D. Miller, *Citizenship and National Identity* (Polity, 2000), while the challenge to this link posed by immigrants, refugees, and asylum seekers is explored in R. Bauböck, *Transnational Citizenship: Membership and Rights in Transnational Migration* (Edward Elgar, 1994); S. Castles and A. Davidson, *Citizenship and Migration: Globalisation and the Politics of Belonging* (Palgrave, 2000); and S. Benhabib, *The Rights of Others: Aliens, Residents and Citizens* (Cambridge University Press, 2004).

Chapter 4

The need to develop a post-national, cosmopolitan form of global citizenship based on rights was articulated in a European context in an influential essay by J. Habermas, 'Citizenship and National Identity: Some Reflections on the Future of Europe', *Praxis International*, 12 (1992), pp. 1–9. A debate, partly inspired by his argument, can be found in K. Hutchings and R. Dannreuther, *Cosmopolitan Citizenship* (Macmillan, 1999). L. Dobson, *Supranational Citizenship* (Manchester University Press, 2006) offers a parallel rights-based argument that is also inspired by developments in the EU. An accessible overview of these debates is provided by D. Heater, *World Citizenship: Cosmopolitan Thinking and Its Opponents* (Continuum, 2002). The cosmopolitan ideal more generally is defended in C. Beitz, *Political Theory and International Relations*, 2nd edn. (Princeton University Press, 1999) and C. Jones, *Global Justice: Defending Cosmopolitanism* (Oxford University Press, 1999).

Rights-based citizenship at the domestic level, and the need for the constitutional entrenchment of rights, is most ably defended in the writings of R. Dworkin, *Freedom's Law: The Moral Reading of the American Constitution* (Oxford University Press, 1996). His ideas are subjected to criticism in J. Waldron, *Law and Disagreement* (Oxford University Press, 1999) and R. Bellamy, *Political Constitutionalism: A Republican Defence of the Constitutionality of Democracy* (Cambridge University Press, 2007).

Chapter 5

R. Dahl, *Democracy and Its Critics* (Yale University Press, 1989) and A. Weale, *Democracy*, 2nd edn. (Palgrave, 2007) offer excellent overviews of various arguments for and against democracy, highlighting its significance for citizenship as a means for securing political equality. C. Pattie, P. Seyd, and P. Whiteley, *Citizenship in Britain: Values, Participation and Democracy* (Cambridge University Press, 2004) looks at changing patterns of political participation in the UK, while P. Norris, *Democratic Phoenix: Reinventing Political Activism* (Cambridge University Press, 2002) and R. Dalton, *Democratic Challenges, Democratic Choices: The Erosion of Support in Advanced Industrial Democracies* (Oxford University Press, 2004) explore participation worldwide. D. Held, *Democracy and the Global Order* (Polity, 1995) defends cosmopolitan democracy, while A. Weale, *Democratic Citizenship in the European Union* (Manchester

University Press, 2006) looks at democratic citizenship in the only transnational context in which it currently applies, as does R. Bellamy, D. Castiglione, and J. Shaw, *Making European Citizens: Civic Inclusion in a Transnational Context* (Palgrave, 2006). C. Hay, *Why We Hate Politics* (Polity, 2007) explores the extent and causes of the current disengagement with politics.

Index

Visit the
VERY SHORT INTRODUCTIONS
Web site

www.oup.co.uk/vsi

➤ **Information** about all published titles

➤ News of **forthcoming books**

➤ **Extracts** from the books, including titles not yet published

➤ **Reviews** and views

➤ **Links** to other **web sites** and main OUP web page

➤ Information about **VSIs in translation**

➤ **Contact** the editors

➤ **Order** other **VSIs** on-line

ARISTOTLE
A Very Short Introduction
Jonathan Barnes

The influence of Aristotle, the prince of philosophers, on the intellectual history of the West is second to none. In this book Jonathan Barnes examines Aristotle's scientific research, his discoveries in logic, his metaphysical theories, his work in psychology, ethics, and politics, and his ideas about art and poetry, placing his teachings in their historical context.

'With compressed verve, Jonathan Barnes displays the extraordinary Versatility of Aristotle, the great systematising empiricist.'

Sunday Times

www.oup.co.uk/isbn/0-19-285408-9

POLITICS
A Very Short Introduction
Kenneth Minogue

In this provocative but balanced essay, Kenneth Minogue discusses the development of politics from the ancient world to the twentieth century. He prompts us to consider why political systems evolve, how politics offers both power and order in our society, whether democracy is always a good thing, and what future politics may have in the twenty-first century.

'This is a fascinating book which sketches, in a very short space, one view of the nature of politics ... the reader is challenged, provoked and stimulated by Minogue's trenchant views.'

Ian Davies, *Talking Politics*

'a dazzling but unpretentious display of great scholarship and humane reflection'

Neil O'Sullivan, University of Hull

www.oup.co.uk/vsi/politics

MACHIAVELLI
A Very Short Introduction
Quentin Skinner

Niccolo Machiavelli taught that political leaders must be prepared to do evil that good may come of it, and his name has been a byword ever since for duplicity and immorality. Is his sinister reputation deserved? In answering this question Quentin Skinner focuses on three major works – *The Prince*, the *Discourses*, and *The History of Florence* – and distils from them an introduction to Machiavelli's doctrines of exemplary clarity.

'Skinner succeeds brilliantly in this interpretation. Clear and concise, this book is the best short introduction of Machiavelli's thought that is available today.'

Felix Gilbert, *Italian Quarterly*

'One can have nothing but praise for the clarity and intelligence of the work'

Mark Phillips, *History of European Ideas*

www.oup.co.uk/isbn/0-19-285407-0